THE
WILDERNESS
WAY
FINDING FREEDOM
IN LIFE'S FRACTURES

DUSTIN KLEINSCHMIDT

The Wilderness Way

© 2025 Dustin Kleinschmidt

All rights reserved. No part of this book may be reproduced, distributed, or transmitted in any form or by any means, including photocopying, recording, or other electronic or mechanical methods, without the prior written permission of the publisher, except in the case of brief quotations embodied in critical reviews and certain other noncommercial uses permitted by copyright law.

Published in the United States by **Normal Pastor co.**
www.thenormalpastor.com

ISBN: 979-8-9934726-0-7

Cover design by Dean Yorimitsu

Interior design by EbookLaunch.com

Scripture quotations marked **NIV** are taken from the *Holy Bible, New International Version®, NIV®.*
Copyright © 1973, 1978, 1984, 2011 by Biblica, Inc.™
Used by permission. All rights reserved worldwide.

For more reflections and resources, visit:
www.dustinkleinschmidt.com

Printed in the United States of America

First Edition

DEDICATION

To every friend, partner, and fellow traveler
who has shared the wilderness road:

Thank you for showing me that hope is found in walking together.

To my family—Riley, Keegan, and Caylee:

You are my greatest joy and the truest glimpse
I've had of God's grace at work in ordinary life.

And to Stacy:

I wouldn't want to journey through this life with anyone else. Your love for Jesus and your selfless heart for others continue to amaze me. You are my anchor, my companion, and my favorite person to laugh with. *You're neat.*

Blessed are those whose strength is in You, whose hearts are set on the journey.

They travel through dry valleys and find them filled with springs. They go from strength to strength until they see God in full view.

Adapted from Psalm 84:5–7

Contents

INTRODUCTION: i

I. Welcome to the Wilderness 1

    1. Wilderness Everywhere 3

    2. The Long Way Around 13

    3. The Sound of Silence 26

II. Why the Wilderness 43

    4. What in the Wilderness?! 45

    5. Cycles, Circles, and Self-Sabotage 62

III. Walking the Wilderness 79

    6. Faithful Is Fruitful 81

    7. Don't Go Solo 96

    8. Holding On to Wholeness 111

IV. Wonder of the Wilderness 129

    9. The Shimmer in the Shadows 131

    10. An Oasis in the Wilderness 146

    11. The Long Way Home 160

Epilogue 173

An Invitation 176

SCRIPTURE REFERENCES 177

About the Author 179

ACKNOWLEDGMENTS 180

NON-BIBLICAL CITATIONS 181

INTRODUCTION:

Learning to See Differently

This is not the book I wanted to write. If I'm being honest, I'd rather write about something lighter—like church health strategies or how you can have everything you ever wanted in three easy steps. I'd rather focus on how everything eventually works out, how faith smooths the edges and resolves the pain. I'd rather tell you that if you just believe enough, pray enough, or obey enough, things will make sense. But that's not my story. And I'd bet it's not yours either.

What I've come to realize—through my own disorientation, doubt, and wandering—is that the wilderness isn't the exception. It's the backdrop of the whole human story. It's not where we get lost, it's where we find out who we really are. And more importantly, it's where we find out who God really is. But getting there requires a willingness to see everything with fresh eyes.

This isn't a book of answers. It's not a roadmap to get you out of the hard places. If you're looking for a formula to bypass grief, avoid disappointment, or speed through the waiting, this probably isn't the book for you. But if you're looking for someone to sit with you in the questions—to help you understand the frustrations as formation, to walk alongside you with honesty and hope—then maybe this is exactly where you need to be.

I should probably say this up front: I'm not a biblical scholar. This book isn't a systematic study of suffering. It's not a nuanced theological treatise, and I'm certainly not writing from the depths of personal tragedy. Honestly, I've had it pretty easy compared to many. My purpose is simply to integrate what I believe is true from Scripture with what I've lived…and with what I've walked through alongside people who've wandered in the gray, wrestled in the silence, and held on to faith through heartache. This is not an expert's manual. It's a companion's voice—offering a different lens through which to see the journey.

I wrote this because I got tired of pretending. Tired of performing. Tired of acting like the life of faith should always feel victorious. The truth is, sometimes we believe deeply and still feel disappointed. Sometimes we trust God and still feel like we're falling apart. Sometimes the miracle doesn't come. And sometimes it does—but not in the way we hoped. This book is about seeing these places differently—the places where things are both beautiful and broken. Where we see glimpses of the Promised Land but still wake up in the wilderness. It's about learning to live in the tension between now and not yet, between rescue and longing, between grace and grit. It's about holding space for sorrow and celebration to sit side by side.

We all instinctively know that the world isn't quite right. You may have learned personally that everything can change in an instant. It doesn't matter if you're rich or poor, young or old, struggle is never far away. Maybe you feel it in the quiet hum of anxiety—that undercurrent that never quite disappears, even in your best moments. Maybe it's in the unexpected breaking of trusted things—the unraveling of relationships that once felt unshakable, the creeping weight of suffering that tries to seep into every corner of life. Or maybe it's in those gut-punch moments, when everything you thought was stable is suddenly gone, leaving you standing in the remains of what once was.

One phone call, one diagnosis, one wrong turn, and life becomes unrecognizable. And even if we manage to sidestep the worst of life's tragedies, we won't escape death—none of us will. It remains undefeated. No matter how much we try to control things, sooner or later, this life catches up with us. And if we're honest, most of what we do in life is an attempt to keep suffering at bay. We pour time, energy, and resources into making life more secure, more comfortable, more predictable. We work hard to create a sense of control, to keep the really hard stuff at arm's length. We chase safety, build systems, and make plans, all in an effort to outrun those wilderness moments. But no matter how hard we try, the wilderness is unavoidable.

Before We Move Forward

Yes, I fully believe God is in control. Yes, He loves us and is leading us. Yes, Jesus is King, and He *is* making all things new.

But maybe before we rush to that hope, we must be willing to reconsider our relationship with reality itself. Maybe before we try to explain it, fix it, or force meaning into it, we need to sit with the weight of it. We don't like to do that (I definitely don't). We want to jump to the part where everything makes sense, where suffering is wrapped in a neat theological bow, where we can say, "God has a plan," and "in all things God works for the good of those who love him, who have been called according to his purpose," and then move on.

But that's not how wilderness works.

Israel didn't step into the desert and immediately see its purpose. They wandered, questioned, struggled, and rebelled. Some days they trusted. Many days they doubted. They didn't know how long it would last or what was coming next. That's where we live. And if we don't first acknowledge the reality of the wilderness for what it truly is, we'll spend our lives fighting it instead of learning to walk through it.

We tend to think of the wilderness as a tough season—those times when life feels uncertain, painful, or directionless. And while that's true, I think it requires a more fundamental shift in perspective. I am convinced that life in this world is the wilderness. And the Bible? It's full of wilderness, too.

- Israel wandered for forty years in the wilderness after being freed from slavery, struggling to trust God, wrestling with fear and doubt.

- Jesus was led by the Spirit into the wilderness, where He fasted for forty days and faced temptation from Satan.

- Hagar was cast out into the wilderness with her son Ishmael, where she thought they would die—until God provided water and a promise.

- Elijah ran into the wilderness when he was overwhelmed and exhausted, collapsing under a tree and asking God to let him die—until an angel showed up with food and a reminder that he wasn't alone.

- David fled into the wilderness, running for his life, where he learned to trust God in the hidden and desperate places.
- John the Baptist lived in the wilderness, preparing the way for Jesus and showing that sometimes the wilderness is where God speaks the loudest.
- Paul spent years in the wilderness after encountering Jesus, being reshaped before stepping into his calling.
- The early church lived as exiles, spiritual wanderers, walking through the wilderness of a broken world and longing for their true home.

Over and over, the wilderness isn't just a place—it's the space between rescue and home. A place of waiting, refining, testing, and transformation. And that's where we are.

We'll take this journey slowly. Not to solve it, but to see it clearly. To pay attention. To remember that God has always met His people in the wilderness—not just to test them, but to be with them and to draw them to Himself. That pattern is all over Scripture. The wilderness is not failure: It is formation.

Maybe you've spent your life trying to avoid pain, as I have. But pain still found me. It showed up early: a broken family, an abusive stepfather, an addiction to pornography—all before I even met Jesus. Then I met Him, experienced grace, and fell into the trap of thinking if I did everything right if I followed the rules and stayed faithful—life may be hard, but not HARD. And for a while, it worked. Or I thought it did.

But the wilderness has a way of breaking through even our best defenses. Loss. Betrayal. Sickness. Doubt. Grief. They come looking for us and those we love whether we're ready or not. We bob and weave, trying to pray our way out. Work our way out. Numb our way out. And still, we end up. in the desert. Still aching. Still wondering if this is what life is supposed to feel like. If that's you, you're not alone.

Recently I walked through another one of these seasons where everything felt like it was falling apart. And I don't mean the dramatic kind of falling apart where you hit rock bottom and then bounce back stronger. I mean the kind where things start quietly unraveling, one thread at a time. Where you're still showing up, still doing all the things, but inside you feel like you're barely holding it together. And maybe no one even notices—even *you* don't always notice. Maybe you've become so good at managing your wilderness that people think you're thriving. But deep down, you know the truth. You're exhausted. You're tired of pretending. You're tired of trying to outrun something that keeps finding you.

The wilderness doesn't care about our title, our income, our Instagram presence, or our theology degree. It comes for all of us. And sometimes it stays longer than we ever imagined it could. But what if it's not a detour? What if we need to rethink our entire understanding of what it means to follow God? What if the wilderness is where we stop striving long enough to hear God again—not in the thunder or fire, but in the whisper?

This book unfolds like a song—not with neat verses and choruses, but with movements that weave together, themes that return and deepen, melodies that echo and build. Because that's how transformation works. It doesn't follow our tidy timelines or respect our section breaks. It circles back. It revisits old wounds with new grace. It offers glimpses of hope, then asks us to walk through another valley. It forms us not through linear progression, but through the patient repetition of trust.

We'll begin by seeing the wilderness for what it truly is—not an interruption to spiritual life, but the very landscape where it unfolds. We'll enter the stories of those who walked this path before us—Israel, Elijah, Hagar, Jesus—and find ourselves in their footsteps. We'll wrestle with the hard questions most of us carry but are afraid to say out loud: If God loves us, why do we suffer? Why does He allow such deep loss, grief, or silence? We won't try to tidy them up or offer easy answers, but we will walk with courage into the darkness and ask God to meet us there.

As we move deeper into this wilderness life, we'll explore what it means to live faithfully when nothing is easy, when prayers seem to echo into silence, and when strength feels like a distant memory. We'll talk about staying present, about what to do when you're barely holding it together, about rhythms that anchor you—not because they fix everything, but because they remind you that you're not alone. We'll lean into lament and rest, into receiving manna when we wanted meat.

And finally, we'll lift our eyes just enough to see what's ahead. Not resolution—the wilderness doesn't end with everything wrapped up in a bow. But glimpses. Moments when the light breaks through the canopy and we remember that there's more coming.

We'll talk about how to hold joy and grief in the same hands, how to become grounded people of hope—men and women who don't ignore the pain but believe God is still doing something beautiful in the middle of it. We'll look at how we carry each other through the wilderness, and how, even in dry places, we can become springs of life for one another.

The wilderness may break us, but it also forms us. Prepares us. Teaches us how to walk again. And sometimes—if we're willing to shift our understanding—it teaches us how to sing.

My Hope for Us

My hope isn't that you walk away from this book with answers, tidy theology, or a handle on suffering—but that you feel seen. That, in some strange and sacred way, these words help you discover a new way of viewing your own wilderness. That you feel less alone.

And more than that, I pray you encounter the presence of God—not just the idea of Him, but His actual nearness. I hope this book becomes an altar, not a textbook. A place to bring your honest self and find that He welcomes you. Wherever you find yourself in the journey—questioning, clinging, collapsing, or catching your breath—I want you to hear this clearly: You are not forgotten. You are not disqualified. You are not abandoned—even here, He is preparing you.

This may not be the book I wanted to write. But it's the one I needed. And maybe it's the one you need, too.

Welcome to the wilderness.

Here's what I've discovered: We are not wilderness survivors, trying to endure until rescue comes. We are Kingdom carriers, walking together toward home, learning to thrive with hope on the horizon. Let's learn to see it differently together.

Before we dive into our own stories—before we name our struggles and map our wandering—maybe we should start somewhere else. Because the truth is, if you've felt lost in the wilderness, you're in good company. This isn't a modern phenomenon, a consequence of our broken world, or evidence that something has gone uniquely wrong with your life. The wilderness has been the backdrop of God's story from the very beginning.

From the garden to the exile, from Egypt to the Promised Land, from the manger to the cross—the people of God have always known what it means to live in the in-between. To wait. To wander. To trust when they couldn't see the path ahead. Your wilderness isn't a detour from God's plan—it's woven into the very fabric of how He works. And maybe, if we can learn to understand that differently, it will change everything about how we walk through it.

I. Welcome to the Wilderness

"Not all those who wander are lost."
— *J.R.R. Tolkien, The Fellowship of the Ring*

1. Wilderness Everywhere

Struggle Through the Whole Story

"Remember how the Lord your God led you all the way in the wilderness these forty years, to humble and test you in order to know what was in your heart..." (Deuteronomy 8:2).

Unraveling

As soon as I got in my car after the elders meeting, I said to myself, "I don't see any way forward." That moment marked the beginning of the end of my role serving in the church I had loved deeply and poured so much into. This was my second stint on staff. I was originally hired by the founding pastor in 2011 to oversee spiritual growth. It was a big move for my family from California to Texas and a significant transition for me—from the West Coast church I had grown up into a young, thriving church in a rapidly growing community.

The first year was incredible. Everything felt fresh. The church grew, I grew, our family grew. But over time, I started having concerns about the senior pastor and how leadership was viewed and exercised. Unfortunately, my concerns were often downplayed or dismissed outright. At the time, I felt like God was encouraging me to stay, trust Him, and continue serving and supporting the church. So I did. I served for the next six years—frustrated but faithful.

In 2017, after significant prayer and conversations with trusted advisors, my wife and I felt like God was leading us to step into planting a church about thirty minutes away. With a small group of families and the blessing—but limited involvement—of our home church, we set out.

The journey was challenging but deeply rewarding. We had a faithful core group and a shared heart to serve the community and show them Jesus. For three years, we did just that—investing deeply in one another and in our community. Then the dream was interrupted by a little thing called COVID. Everything we had built was suddenly tested in ways we never could have anticipated. Over time, it became clear the weight of continuing was falling on too few families—and that burden was wearing us all down. So we made the painful decision to close it down.

As we processed yet another transition, something unexpected happened: I was invited to return and help lead the church we had previously been part of into a new future. Since I had left, they had gone through the loss of the founding pastor due to moral failure and the resignation of all their elders, an extremely difficult (and expensive) building project, and that pesky pandemic. It was the trifecta of things that kill churches.

I was thrilled at the opportunity—full of hope for what could be. But almost before my keycard had even unlocked the door, everything went sideways. It felt like crisis after crisis. The leadership team was burned out and overwhelmed. A disgruntled former leader took a group of people—along with two staff members—and planted a church nearby. We walked through the painful process of transitioning beloved staff and leaders out of their roles. Budget cuts forced difficult decisions, including pay decreases and staff layoffs. Some of the younger leaders were growing impatient, pushing for faster change than I believed was healthy. And the congregation—worn down by past wounds and constant change—was cautious, fatigued, and struggling to trust again.

Those four years were the most painful and isolating years I had ever experienced. The breaking point came that Saturday morning when I sat with our elders and listened to a couple of the younger leaders express that they no longer wanted to follow our leadership—and that perhaps it was time for all of us to move on. My heart sank—not just because of their words, the sense of betrayal, or their lack of confidence in my leadership, but because in that moment, I fully realized how overwhelmed, frustrated, and exhausted I had become. I realized I couldn't be who they needed me to be. And worse—for the first time in my life—I didn't want to be.

I didn't want to be a pastor.

I didn't want to lead.

I didn't want to navigate the endless challenges, personalities, and expectations anymore.

The very work that had brought me life and excitement for over twenty years now brought only exhaustion and pain. I was done with ministry—not just in that role, not just in that church, but maybe forever.

As I drove home that day, I was flooded with questions. What did I do wrong? What will I do now?

And then, the deeper, more painful questions surfaced: Am I a failure? Am I the problem? If I'm not in ministry, then who am I? What am I worth? These questions consumed me for the next twelve months.

That was the beginning of a season where nothing made sense. Where identity crumbled. Where purpose felt distant and silence felt like abandonment. In many ways, I think I'm still in it. Still waking up some days unsure what all of this is forming in me. Still wondering what's next. Still waiting.

And maybe that's part of the point. I'm learning that life, while beautiful and meaningful, is also undeniably hard. Beneath all the good, we know deep down it isn't how it's supposed to be. But maybe the discomfort isn't just brokenness. Maybe it's also mercy—the kind that won't let us settle for less than we were made for. And that's why we need to talk about the wilderness.

Wilderness Everywhere

There is wilderness everywhere in Scripture. It is the backdrop of some of the most pivotal moments in the story of God's people. It's where Israel wandered for forty years, where Elijah collapsed under a broom tree, where Hagar wept in despair, where David hid in caves, and where John the Baptist made his home. It's where Paul was shaped before his ministry began. It's where Jesus fasted, fought temptation, and walked out of the desert filled with the Spirit's power. The wilderness is not just a setting in the Bible—it is woven into its very fabric.

From the moment Adam and Eve were thrust outside Eden, humanity has been wandering east of wholeness—longing for home, trying to find our way back. Genesis 3 was the first exile, the first wilderness. What was once effortless communion with God became toil, sweat, pain, and separation. Eden was behind them, and the wilderness stretched out before them.

The wilderness was full of war, bloodshed, and fractured lives. It was where Cain murdered his brother, where humanity built towers to the heavens in an effort to make a name for themselves. It was where the world spiraled into such violence that God sent a flood to cleanse it, only for Noah's descendants to return to the same patterns of power and rebellion.

The wilderness was a place where everyone did what is right in their own eyes. It was where kings enslaved, where leaders slaughtered, where sin brought devastation. It was the backdrop of exile, struggle, testing, and transformation. It was where humanity wrestled with God, with itself, and with the uncertainty of what came next.

Yet even here, God was not absent. He did not remove the wilderness, but He did not abandon His people in it either. He was there—sometimes unseen, sometimes silent, but always present in the dust and the hunger, the questions and the wandering. The wilderness was not just a wasteland—it was the proving ground of faith.

The Exodus Cycle

The story of Scripture follows this same rhythm: a people in exile, a longing for home, and a God who meets them in the in-between. It's not just an ancient narrative—it's our story, too. Israel's story is our story. It is a picture of the journey every follower of Jesus must take.

SLAVERY

First, there was slavery—Israel bound in Egypt, crying out under the weight of oppression. For generations, God's people had known nothing but labor and chains, their identity reduced to what they could produce for their masters. Egypt had shaped them–physically, mentally, and spiritually. Their cries for deliverance were desperate, but when freedom finally came, they struggled to walk in it.

This is the nature of slavery—it not only confines the body but warps the soul. Even after God set them free, Egypt still lived inside of them. They longed for what was familiar, even if it had been brutal. They had been shaped by years of bondage, conditioned to survive under the weight of oppression.

THE WILDERNESS

God's plan was not just to bring them out of Egypt—He needed to bring Egypt out of them. The habits of slavery had to be unlearned. The false securities of their oppressors had to be stripped away.

The wilderness was a place of hunger and thirst, of wandering and wondering if God was still near. It was filled with grumbling voices and shattered expectations, golden calves and fiery serpents. Every step forward seemed to cost something, and the landscape itself echoed with questions: Why this way? Why so long? Why so hard?

And yet, this was the road God chose on purpose. Not the shortest path, but the desert road—where the echoes of Egypt could be drawn out of their bones, where slavery's grip on their identity could finally be broken. The wilderness wasn't just a detour; it was the place where the past was exposed, the soul was laid bare, and everything false had to die.

The wilderness exposed what Israel had been clinging to, peeling back the layers of their false securities. It revealed the idols they didn't even know they worshiped—comfort, control, certainty, approval. But it was also where they came to the end of themselves.

THE PROMISED LAND

Finally, there was the Promised Land—the fulfillment, the arrival, the homecoming. For forty years, they had wandered, learning the hard way that God was their only true source. And despite their failures—their grumbling, their doubts, their outright rebellion—He was faithful. He brought them to a land flowing with milk and honey. Not because they had earned it, but because He had promised it.

For Israel, stepping into the land was not the end. There were still battles to fight, strongholds to take, and choices to make. But they had arrived, and that alone was evidence of God's unwavering faithfulness. It was all grace.

Yet it was the wilderness that had formed them. There, God stripped away their false securities and taught them how to live as free people. The wilderness wasn't a detour; it was the path.

Moses' Reflection

"Remember how the Lord your God led you all the way in the wilderness these forty years, to humble and test you in order to know what was in your heart, whether or not you would keep his commands. He humbled you, causing you to hunger and then feeding you with manna, which neither you nor your ancestors had known, to teach you that man does not live on bread alone but on every word that comes from the mouth of the Lord" (Deuteronomy 8:2–3).

This was the wilderness theology Moses wanted them to carry forward: "God didn't just sustain you in the wilderness—He shaped you." The wilderness wasn't just a test of survival. It was a test of the heart. God allowed their hunger—not because He was cruel, but because He was teaching them how to trust.

And when He did provide? It came in a form they didn't expect: manna. Nothing they could manufacture. Nothing they could predict. Just enough for the day. Daily bread by the hand of a daily God.

God humbles us to teach us. He lets us be tested so we'll see what's in us—and what still needs to be formed. And even in their rebellion, God never abandoned them. "Your clothes did not wear out and your feet did not swell during these forty years" (v. 4). Moses said, "Know then in your heart that as a man disciplines his son, so the Lord your God disciplines you" (v. 5.). This wasn't punishment—it was parenting. Formation. Love.

Everything about those forty years was forming them. Exposing what was fragile. Rebuilding what had been warped. Teaching them to depend, to listen, to trust. The wilderness wasn't an accident. It was a classroom. And the same is true for us.

Jesus' Wilderness

Jesus spent time in the wilderness, too. Right after His baptism—right after the Father declared, "This is my beloved Son"—He was led by the Spirit into the desert. No food. No shelter. Just hunger, loneliness, and the voice of the enemy whispering lies.

It's easy to forget that this was the very first step of Jesus' public ministry. Before any miracles, before any sermons, before any calling of disciples —He fasted alone in the desert for forty days. Because even the Son of God did not bypass the wilderness.

The wilderness was a test—not of Jesus' strength, but of His trust in His Father. The enemy came with questions: "If you are the Son of God…" It was the same whisper that had echoed since Eden: "Can you really trust Him?" "Will He actually provide?"

Yet He did not waver. Israel had complained about bread; Jesus held fast to the words of God. Israel had demanded signs; Jesus refused to test the Father. In fact, Jesus answered every lie with Scripture:

"It is written: 'Man shall not live on bread alone, but on every word that comes from the mouth of God'" (Matthew 4:4).

He wasn't just facing temptation—He was walking the same path Israel had walked. But notice the difference: Where they failed, He triumphed; where they grumbled, He trusted.

Running Back to Egypt

Even after all God does for us, we often still find ourselves running back to Egypt. Not literally, but spiritually, emotionally, practically—we run back to what enslaved us. We return to old patterns, old securities. Like Israel, we prefer the familiar bondage to the unfamiliar freedom.

The Golden Calf (Exodus 32)

Moses was on the mountain for forty days. From Israel's perspective, he had been gone too long. So they gathered their gold and forged a new god with their own hands. Not because they had forgotten Yahweh's name, but because they couldn't handle waiting anymore. They needed something visible. Controllable.

We do this, too. When God seems slow, we react. When His timeline stretches beyond our comfort, we take blessings and turn them into idols—careers, relationships, platforms. The golden calf wasn't about theology. It was about fear.

Craving Meat Over Manna (Numbers 11)

God was providing daily. Manna each morning—dependable, nourishing. But over time, it became monotonous. "We remember the fish we ate in Egypt at no cost…" At no cost? They were talking about Egypt—the place of whips and oppression. But now, all they could remember were the flavors.

So they grumbled. They demanded meat. And God gave them exactly what they asked for—quail until it came out of their noses. The place was renamed Kibroth Hattaavah, "the graves of craving."

We get bored with God's ordinary faithfulness. We romanticize our past dysfunctions when the present feels flat. But God's provision isn't meant to entertain us—it's meant to form us.

Refusing the Promised Land (Numbers 13–14)

At the edge of promise, fear took over. The spies saw giants and forgot who they were. "We looked like grasshoppers compared to them." Despite all God has done, they panicked. "Let's go back to Egypt."

When God invites us into uncertainty, we crave guarantees. And when the giants come into view, we convince ourselves that maybe going back wouldn't be so bad after all.

Where Egypt Leads (Jeremiah 7)

What began as grumbling in the wilderness eventually grew into something horrific. After generations of compromise, Israel wasn't just dabbling in idolatry—they were immersed in it. And then we read this: "They have built the high places of Topheth…to burn their sons and daughters in the fire—something I did not command, nor did it enter my mind" (Jeremiah 7:31).

This wasn't some sudden collapse. It was the end result of a slow erosion—a drift that began with fear, impatience, and running back to Egypt.

And if we're paying attention, we see ourselves. Our idols may not be carved from stone, but when we keep running back to our own versions of Egypt—the comfort of busyness, the familiar numbness of screens, the illusion of control—we end up offering our children to endless schedules, absent presence, and lives shaped by unchecked ambition. We don't mean to. But in our striving, we raise a generation shaped more by anxiety than abiding.

The Pattern We Follow

God is not surprised by our failures. He doesn't flinch at our compulsions. The Scriptures call Him "long-suffering" for a reason. His patience is not passive—it's fierce.

It waits.

It invites.

It celebrates every trembling step toward Him.

Think of a child learning to walk. The falls aren't failures—they're formation. The parent doesn't rebuke the stumbles—they cheer for the steps. That's what God does with us in the wilderness. He's not measuring your perfection. He's watching for your trust.

So if you're feeling like you've blown it, hear this: God hasn't left. He's not done. He's not disappointed that you fell. He's delighted that you're still trying to walk. The invitation is simple but not easy: Instead of reacting, choose to reflect. Instead of running to Egypt, run to Him.

That's how to walk through the wilderness: Don't walk it alone. Don't walk it in denial. Don't walk it pretending you're not afraid.

Walk slowly.

Walk honestly.

Walk aware of your patterns.

Walk toward the Presence that refuses to walk away. Because He is here with you—not waiting for you to get it right, but inviting you to see Him rightly.

Delay does not mean denial. The wilderness is not punishment—it's preparation. And the discomfort you feel? It's not evidence of God's absence. It's the sign that you are on the path He's chosen to shape you. We live between Eden lost and the Kingdom coming—the wilderness of the in-between. But God is here. And He is enough.

So don't rush the process. Don't despise the slow. Faithfulness in the wilderness matters more than how quickly you can get through it. This chapter in your life doesn't resolve with escape; it resolves with trust.

2. The Long Way Around

In Between Rescue and Restoration

"All these people were still living by faith when they died… admitting that they were foreigners and strangers on earth. People who say such things show that they are looking for a country of their own… they were longing for a better country—a heavenly one. Therefore God is not ashamed to be called their God, for he has prepared a city for them" (Hebrews 11:13–16).

Life in Tension

It's a beautiful spring day. I'm sitting outside on the patio of a local coffee shop, warmed by the sun as I write this. The breeze is light. The trees are beginning to bloom. It's that great season where either hot or iced coffee can be the perfect drink.

As I take it all in, these are just a few of the headlines in today's news:

"Dow tumbles 2,000 points."

"Youth soccer coach accused of killing 13-year-old boy."

"Teen fatally stabbed at a track meet in Texas."

"Bolivia floods kill at least 55, affecting nearly 600,000 families."

There it is…

The contrast.

The dissonance.

This warm, peaceful day doesn't match the headlines. The sunlight feels deceptive. Sometimes it's hard to make sense of a world where beauty and brutality live side by side. But that's the world we live in. This is the tension we all carry, whether we want to acknowledge it or not. The messiness of this world isn't distant or theoretical. It's not limited to war zones or international headlines. In the digital age, it shows up on our home pages and news feeds. It even creeps into the most intimate spaces.

In just the past year, within my own circle of friends and family, my wife was knocked off her feet by a virus that left her barely functioning for over three months. I stepped away from full-time ministry, shaking loose more of my identity than I ever anticipated (as shared in Chapter 1). A longtime friend was diagnosed with terminal brain cancer and passed away. Our neighbor was diagnosed with esophageal cancer, and his wife suffered a stroke. And that's just a small sampling.

Then there are the simpler struggles. The ones that don't make the prayer list but still chip away at your soul (and possibly your body). For example, I've had tendonitis in my elbow for months—not a tragedy, just obnoxious (and a humbling reminder that I'm not as young as I used to be). It makes simple things harder, more frustrating. It's also allergy season (fall and spring in Texas), which turns me into a less patient, more irritable version of myself. Nothing catastrophic. Just a slow, low-grade grind.

Someone going 50 in the fast lane—wilderness.

Microwave beeps, food's still cold—wilderness.

Printer jams five minutes before the meeting—wilderness.

Every pen in the drawer is dead—wilderness.

These aren't separate realities. They're all part of the same wilderness life. We tend to think of the wilderness as a specific hardship. A defined season of loss or disorientation. Something that has a clear beginning, a painful middle, and—if we're lucky—a triumphant end. A diagnosis. A job loss. A breakup. A crisis of faith. But maybe it's more than that?

What if the wilderness isn't just found in the big disruptions of life—but also in the quiet, constant annoyances that follow us even on the good days? What if it's not just the trauma or the tragedy, but the accumulation of the global, the personal, and the painfully ordinary that unveils the deeper truth? That we're not home. That something's off. That even when the coffee is warm and the sky is clear, something inside us still groans for more.

We all think we have a plan. We all have expectations for how life should or will go. We all picture a version of the future where things unfold on schedule—our health holds steady, our finances grow, our relationships deepen, our faith matures at a consistent upward angle. It's a good plan. Logical. Manageable. Comfortable.

And then… it doesn't happen. Surprise—your 401(k) isn't as robust as you thought. Your health isn't as bulletproof as you hoped (even after all the kale salads, vitamins, and Apple Watch badges). That relationship you assumed would always be steady starts to drift. The job security you once had disappears. The spiritual clarity you had gained begins to blur. You don't have the control you thought you did.

The great philosopher Mike Tyson once said, "Everyone has a plan until they get punched in the face." And honestly? I think that's one of the more compelling truths we can embrace about this wilderness life. We make plans. Life lands a punch. And suddenly, we're not walking the well-marked path we carefully mapped out—we're stumbling through terrain we never expected, trying to figure out which way is forward. Trying to figure out who we even are now.

This is the wilderness. Not a temporary inconvenience. Not a metaphor for a few hard weeks. But the actual terrain we walk every day—between rescue and home. Between what God has already done and what He has yet to finish. So if the world feels a little too heavy, or your body feels too tired, or your soul is restless for reasons you can't quite name…you're not broken. You're just here.

I know that might sound bleak—like something out of a '90s emo song. But that's not the heart behind it. This isn't fatalism. It's not pessimism wrapped in spiritual language. It's just…reality. And recognizing reality—naming it for what it is—actually helps us live differently. Too often, we're caught off guard when life feels hard. When suffering comes. When things don't work the way they're supposed to. There's this quiet expectation that if we do things right, we'll be spared from the mess. That hardship is the exception, not the rule. Not only is that not accurate, it's also not biblical. But it is often the unspoken undercurrent of Christianity, especially in the West.

Should we really be surprised? We live east of Eden, after all. The ground is hard. Birth is painful. Loss is inevitable. Pain is part of the fabric for now. We were made for wholeness, but we live in fracture. And pretending otherwise only makes it harder when the truth comes crashing in. I have truly come to believe that this life is our wilderness—not just a season.

For followers of Jesus, our story is one of rescue and promise. We've been delivered from slavery to sin—that part is already done. One day, we'll arrive home in the new heavens and new earth—that promise is secure. But right now? We're in between. Living in the already-but-not-yet.

This middle ground is the wilderness.

The space between redemption and restoration.

The place where manna falls just enough for today, and the Promised Land is still just a glimpse on the horizon.

It's where there are beautiful sunrises and chronic pain that won't go away. Where a new baby is born while someone else buries their father. Where there's laughter at the dinner table and silence in a strained marriage—sometimes in the same home. Where your child takes their first steps the same week your friend gets a cancer diagnosis. Where dreams come true and depression still lingers. Where church feels like home one week and a source of deep hurt the next. Where prayers are both answered and unanswered—sometimes in the same breath.

It's not all darkness, and it's not all light. It's both. At once. Every day. The wilderness is this strange in-between space where joy and sorrow live side by side. Where hope is real—but so is grief.

This is the tension of life here. The ache of living in a world that has been rescued but not yet restored. The story isn't over, but the waiting can feel long. And some days, we wonder if we're going to make it.

So yes—this life is the wilderness. Welcome. Enjoy your stay. That's not resignation, it's reorientation. It's how we begin to adjust our expectations so we can actually live well here. We stop asking the wilderness to be something it was never meant to be, and we start learning how to walk through it with honesty and hope.

The Bible often describes life this way—not as something settled and polished, but as a journey. A pilgrimage. In Psalm 84, the psalmist says, "Blessed are those whose strength is in you, whose hearts are set on pilgrimage…They go from strength to strength, till each appears before God in Zion."

It's a long road. Sometimes the path is joyful. Other times, it winds through valleys of dryness and grief. But the movement is what matters. The direction. The fact that we're not wandering aimlessly…we're headed somewhere.

Stanley Hauerwas, a theologian known for challenging the Western church's addiction to comfort and control, once wrote that the wilderness "ought not to appear to contemporary Christians in America as a foreboding and frightening possibility but as an opportunity to rediscover the excitement and spirit, but also the rigorous discipline, of faithful itinerancy." [1]

In other words, we need to stop expecting stability and start learning how to live like travelers—people who know they're not home yet. "Faithful itinerancy" means learning to walk through life with a pilgrim's heart. It's about letting go of the illusion that this world will ever be perfectly settled or safe, and instead embracing a posture of movement, trust, and dependency. It's traveling light. It's holding loosely to what we gain and what we lose. It's staying rooted not in outcomes or destinations, but in the God who walks with us day by day.

This is the invitation of the wilderness: to stop grasping for permanence and instead learn how to be faithful on the move. It's learning to "bob and weave." To carry less. To walk slower. To lean deeper into God's provision—even when it's not what we asked for. Especially when it's not what we asked for. It's a shift in posture—one that opens us up to what Scripture has been saying all along.

But if this life really is the wilderness—if it's not just sprinkled with hardship but fundamentally shaped by it—then we have to ask: *Why?* Why is the ground so hard? Why is the frustration so constant? Why does joy even seem to arrive with something heavy trailing behind it?

---

[1] Hauerwas, Stanley. 1997. Wilderness Wanderings: Probing Twentieth-Century Theology and Philosophy. Boulder, CO: Westview Press.

To understand the wilderness, we have to go back to the beginning.

How the Story Goes

East of Eden: The Fracture That Shaped the World

In Genesis 1 and 2, the world was whole. There was no wilderness—just a garden. God walked with His people. Everything was in rhythm. There was peace, beauty, intimacy, and abundance. But in Genesis 3, everything fractured. Adam and Eve reached for what God withheld, believing the lie that maybe He wasn't good—maybe He was holding out. And when they ate from the tree, everything unraveled.

Their relationship with God fractured; they hid from Him. Their relationship within themselves broke; they felt shame. Their relationship with each other splintered; they blamed. And their relationship with the ground, the very earth they were made from, became cursed.

"Cursed is the ground because of you; through painful toil you will eat food from it all the days of your life. It will produce thorns and thistles for you... By the sweat of your brow you will eat your food until you return to the ground" (Genesis 3:17–19),

Everything was harder now. Everything resisted them. Creation groaned under the weight of the curse. The garden was closed off, and they stepped into a world that will never again be what it was meant to be.

That's where we live—the world we inherited. The terrain of the wilderness isn't just metaphorical—it's theological. It's the consequence of sin's entrance into creation. Not just personal sin, but a cosmic fracture that rippled into every corner of existence. Nothing was left untouched. This is why the world is both stunningly beautiful and profoundly broken. Why relationships bring both joy and pain. Why our bodies heal and decay. Why we can worship deeply and still wrestle with doubt. Why there's wonder and sorrow in the same breath. It's the Genesis 3 effect. We live in the shadow of the garden—east of Eden—and the wilderness has become the backdrop of every human life.

Between Rescue and Home: The Already-But-Not-Yet

For followers of Jesus, there's another layer to the story. Jesus came to restore what was broken, reconcile what was fractured, and remake the world in its Eden-intended design. Through His death and resurrection, we've been rescued. We've been freed from slavery to sin. We are no longer under condemnation. We've been brought out of Egypt.

But we're not in the Promised Land yet.

There's a tension the New Testament invites us to live in—what theologians call the "already-but-not-yet." We've already been saved, already been adopted, already received the Spirit… and yet we're still waiting. Still groaning. Still longing for home.

Paul describes it like this: *"I consider that our present sufferings are not worth comparing with the glory that will be revealed in us…the whole creation has been groaning as in the pains of childbirth right up to the present time…we ourselves, who have the firstfruits of the Spirit, groan inwardly as we wait eagerly for our adoption to sonship, the redemption of our bodies"* (Romans 8:18–23),

We groan because we're not there yet. And that groaning? It's not a failure of faith—it's a sign of it. It means we remember Eden, even if we've never seen it. It means we know deep down that this isn't how it's supposed to be. And we long for the day when everything's made new. But until then—we wander. Not aimlessly. But with open eyes and heavy hearts, knowing we're not home yet.

Groundhog Day

The wilderness rhythm we explored in the previous chapter—slavery, wilderness, promised land—isn't just Israel's ancient story. It's the pattern every believer walks through. We've been rescued from slavery to sin, and we're promised a home in the new creation. But right now? We're in the wilderness of the in-between. And the question isn't whether we'll face the same struggles Israel did—it's whether we'll learn what they were meant to learn in the wandering. The writer of Hebrews 13:14 puts it plainly: *"For here we do not have an enduring city, but we are looking for the city that is to come."*

That's a reality check. Everything we're building here, everything we cling to, everything we fight to protect—it's not enduring. The jobs we pour ourselves into. The financial plans we obsess over. The homes we renovate. The social status we chase. The security we think we've earned. Even the legacies we hope to leave behind. None of it lasts. It might be beautiful. It might even be meaningful. But it's not permanent. Jesus once called it "wood, hay, and stubble"—things that burn, not things that build eternity.

We are surrounded by temporary things that pretend to be eternal. And the longer we live, the more we see it. A diagnosis can unravel your five-year plan. A phone call can shift your entire family's future. A market crash can erase decades of work.

Hebrews doesn't say the world is meaningless. It just says it's not the point. We're looking for a better city. The one that's still to come. The discomfort we feel here—it's not a flaw in the system. It's a signal. A holy restlessness that reminds us not to settle for what was never meant to satisfy.

So yes—love what you've been given. Steward it well. Celebrate it. Grieve it when it's lost. But don't expect it to last forever. That's what makes the wilderness so frustrating…and so freeing. Frustrating, because nothing holds. Freeing, because we can stop pretending that it should. We're pilgrims. Travelers. Strangers in a land that isn't ours. Paul echoes the same truth reminding us that "*…our citizenship is in heaven. And we eagerly await a Savior from there, the Lord Jesus Christ*" (Philippians 3:20).

This is the thread that runs through the entire biblical narrative. It's everywhere—as if God is whispering (and sometimes shouting), "You are a people on the way. Not settled. Not home. Not finished."

So we can stop chasing permanence in temporary places. Stop expecting lasting peace from a world that was never designed to deliver it. Instead, we can live with open hands. Eyes lifted. Hearts that are still in the fight—but no longer fooled by the illusion that this is home. This is not the city. This is the road. And it is not enduring. Something better is coming.

This isn't just good theology—it's our lived reality. It's why you can love Jesus deeply and still feel a little lost. Why your faith can be sincere, and you can still feel like you're wandering. Why seasons of joy don't erase the frustrations beneath the surface. It's not because you're doing something wrong. It's because this is where we all live. And that has to become the lens we view all of life through. It has to shape how we read Scripture. How we pray. How we think about pain and confusion—not as proof of God's absence, but as places where He draws near in ways we don't always expect. More quietly. More slowly. But just as real.

The wilderness doesn't mean God is gone. It means He's walking with us in ways we're still learning how to see.

This way of seeing doesn't minimize pain—it validates it. It explains why we feel tired. Why we feel out of place. Why we feel like something is missing, even on the best days. But it also anchors us in a bigger story. None of this is pointless. The waiting isn't wasted.

The wilderness has always been the place where God forms His people. That's where trust is grown. Where faith is forged. Where illusions fall away. Where we remember who we are—and who He is. So yes—this life is the wilderness. And if you're just starting to see that…

Welcome.

You're not alone. And Scripture has been telling us this all along.

Mitigating the Mess

Drive through almost any suburban neighborhood in America and you'll see something fascinating: The wilderness has become well-manicured. Neatly trimmed, weedless grass. Lush flower beds. Strategically placed trees. Bark mulch, landscape lighting, and seasonal wreaths.

The only places that look even remotely wild are the homes that aren't lorded over by an HOA. What could be overgrown and untamed has been wrestled into submission—tamed by an army of lawn-care professionals, mountains of fertilizer, and an ocean of weed and feed. I know how much I spend just to keep my own yard presentable. And I'm not even trying to win "Yard of the Month" (though I have).

We've landscaped our lives the same way. We've built a world designed to mitigate the wilderness. We insulate ourselves from discomfort at every turn. Our homes are climate-controlled to the exact degree. Groceries show up at our doorstep—no harvest, no waiting, and often no human interaction. We can numb pain with a single swipe, avoid silence with a scroll, and drown out sorrow with noise on demand. Boredom has been eliminated. Inconvenience has been outsourced. Even our pets sleep on orthopedic beds and eat organic diets that rival what most people in history—or even in the world today—could only dream of.

And to be clear—these comforts aren't necessarily evil. They're often part of God's common grace, the mercy He scatters throughout a fractured world. He sends rain on the just and the unjust (Matthew 5:45).

Good food, medicine, hot showers, warm houses, internet access, distraction when you need to catch your breath. These are not always enemies of faith. They can be blessings. They can be gifts. But when comfort becomes a lifestyle of avoidance—when we use ease as a shield against reality—something happens. The wilderness doesn't go away. We just lose sight of it. We forget where we actually live. We start to believe we're immune to suffering, rather than simply insulated from it.

We've engineered so much of the struggle out of daily life that when real hardship does come, it doesn't just hurt. It undoes us. It disorients us. It shocks us. Because deep down, we thought we had escaped from pain. But we never did. We just forgot that we were still in the wilderness.

It's a fallen and fractured world, full of fallen and fractured people. And pretending otherwise doesn't protect us from it—it just makes the pain feel like failure when it finally arrives. We groan because something in us knows: This isn't it. The pain, the fragility, and the losses feel off because they are.

Our souls remember Eden even if our minds don't. There's this mysterious ache built into us—a longing for something more, even when life is "good." That's the tension of the wilderness: beauty and brokenness, side by side. And when suffering comes, most of us don't know what to do with it. We assume something went wrong… that maybe we're being punished. Maybe we're the exception, the ones God forgot to protect.

The wilderness doesn't care about your résumé. It doesn't skip over the faithful. It comes for everyone. Paul understood this better than most. His life was a mosaic of hardship—beatings, imprisonments, three shipwrecks (maybe stay off the ocean, Paul), betrayal, sleepless nights, hunger, anxiety, and deep loneliness. He didn't talk about suffering from a distance—he lived in it, walked with it, bore it in his own body. And yet, he writes: *"For our light and momentary troubles are achieving for us an eternal glory that far outweighs them all"* (2 Corinthians 4:17).

That phrase "light and momentary" isn't dismissive. It's a contrast of scale. The word "light" (*elaphros*) means light in weight, not in intensity. And "momentary" (*parautika*) means temporary—fleeting, not permanent. Paul isn't saying it doesn't hurt. He's saying compared to the weight of glory, it doesn't even tip the scale. This isn't a spiritual bypass (we'll talk more about that in a later chapter). The truth is, Paul stared the wilderness in the face and chose to keep walking. He bled and broke and wept—and still believed there was more.

So we must shift our expectations—not so we become cynical or numb, but so we stop being blindsided when the hard days come. Because they will come. The wilderness will find us. And when it does, we don't have to panic. We don't have to assume something's gone wrong. We just have to remember where we are—and, more importantly, who's walking with us through it.

God doesn't avoid the wilderness. He doesn't wait for us to clean ourselves up or climb out of the pit. Over and over again in Scripture, we see a God who meets people right in the middle of their collapse—not with shame, but with sustenance. Not with lectures, but with bread and rest. Not with quick fixes, but with quiet provision. The psalms echo this same cry—this mix of despair and hope that only wilderness seasons seem to surface: *"My soul is downcast within me… Deep calls to deep in the roar of your waterfalls; all your waves and breakers have swept over me."* (Psalm 42:6–7)

And yet somehow, even in the flood of sorrow, he keeps reaching: *"Why, my soul, are you downcast? Why so disturbed within me? Put your hope in God, for I will yet praise him…"* (Psalm 42:11)

This is what faith often looks like in the wilderness. This is what it looks like to seek God. It's not certainty. Not clarity. But stubborn hope—a belief that God hasn't gone anywhere, even when we can't feel Him.

We'll explore more in Chapter 5 about how to recognize God's voice in the quiet. But for now, maybe it's enough to remember this: God does not despise your collapse. He doesn't rush you through the pain. He feeds. He rests. He waits with you. The wilderness doesn't mean God is far. Sometimes it's the very place He draws closest.

Enjoy Your Stay

Welcome to the wilderness. We are exiles wandering in a foreign land but we aren't alone. The wilderness should not surprise us. We are people living between rescue and home—in the tension of what already is and what is still to come. And the wilderness, as exhausting as it is, is not a sign that something's gone wrong. It's simply where we are.

Faithfulness in the wilderness is not about solving suffering; it's about enduring with honesty. It's not about tying up loose ends or pretending we're okay when we're not; it's naming the ache. It's asking the hard questions. It's waking up and trusting God again, even when nothing feels resolved.

God is not afraid of your grief. He's not intimidated by your doubt. He doesn't flinch at your questions or stand off at a distance waiting for you to pull it together. God wears big boy pants He can handle the full weight of your pain, your confusion, your "I'm barely holding on." More than that—He's present in it. He provides what we need—not always what we want, and rarely in the timing we would prefer, but what we need to take the next step.

Hebrews 11 reminds us that some of the most faithful people who ever lived did not see the fulfillment of the promises in their lifetime. They lived with longing. They died with questions. And still—they were commended for their faith. Not because they reached a finish line, but because they never stopped walking.

That's not failure. That's faith.

That's our calling, too. Pilgrims. Wanderers with a purpose. People whose hearts are set on something more than what we can see right now. The journey is hard—but it's headed somewhere. God never calls us to white-knuckle our way through life. But He does call us—again and again—to hold on. Not because the path is easy, but because the destination is real. Because we are not alone. Because even here, in the dust and the ache and the wandering, God walks with us.

One day, He'll welcome us home. The city He has prepared is still to come. But until then…we keep going. Together. Honest. At times weary. But hopeful. Wilderness people—with hearts set on pilgrimage.

Knowing this is the wilderness—accepting that we're living between rescue and restoration—doesn't silence all the questions. In fact, sometimes it makes them louder. If this really is how life works, if the wilderness is normal rather than exceptional, then why?

Why does the path to the Promised Land have to lead through such barren places? Why can't love be simple, faith be straightforward, obedience bear immediate fruit?

These aren't rebellious questions—they're honest ones. And honest questions deserve honest answers, even when those answers stretch us beyond what feels comfortable. Sometimes the very acceptance of wilderness reality opens the door to deeper wrestling. And maybe that's exactly where God wants to meet us.

3. The Sound of Silence

Where Is God in the Wilderness?

"...And after the fire came a gentle whisper" (1 Kings 19:12).

Marco...?

"Are you being quiet, or am I not listening?"

It's a question I've asked God more times than I can count. Most recently, I was sitting in my usual booth at the local Panera, trying everything I knew to get God to show up—Bible open, new highlighters in hand, Moleskine journal, worship favorites playlist on repeat.

It had been a particularly dry stretch after I stepped away from my role as a pastor. It felt like I'd been wandering the wilderness without a map—and, more painfully, without much sense that God was walking it with me. No clear answers. No comforting direction. Not even a whisper of reassurance.

I'm usually okay with walking through hard things. I'm idealistic enough (and maybe dumb enough) to think I can make it happen—push through, find a solution, figure it out. I can endure a lot, but what I need most is to know God is in it with me. I don't just want to survive something hard—I want to know I'm not alone in it. That He's still near. Still speaking.

The silence made it really hard to tell. And silence—real silence—isn't neutral. It messes with you. Don't believe me? Try this: The next time someone walks up to you and says hi or asks a question, just stay quiet. Don't respond, just stare at them blankly and see what happens. It makes people squirm. It'll make you squirm.

Silence invites all the questions you thought you'd outgrown. You start wondering if you did something wrong—if you missed some critical direction. If you've been disqualified, dismissed, or abandoned. And when you can't hear God, you eventually start to lose track of your own voice, too.

It feels a little like playing Marco Polo. If you've ever played, you know the feeling—eyes closed in a pool, calling out "Marco" again and again, straining and waiting for someone—anyone—to answer "Polo." You're reaching, guessing, groping your way toward someone who always seems just out of reach.

That's what God's silence felt like for me.

In all the noise of that year—the emotional noise, the vocational unraveling, the spiritual disorientation—God was conspicuously quiet. There was only one moment I felt like He spoke clearly. It was about two months after I had resigned. I was overwhelmed, trying to figure out what was next, what I was supposed to do, how we were going to pay the bills. And then, in the middle of the agitation and anxiety, I heard something. Not audibly, but unmistakably. A thought that didn't sound like mine because I would never suggest something so impractical, so frustratingly unstrategic. God simply said, "You serve and trust Me to provide."

That was it.

And I remember thinking—maybe even saying out loud—"Well, that's a dumb idea."

He didn't respond. And He hasn't added much since, at least not with that same clarity. Just silence. So that one sentence became the filter for basically everything. It's the guiding voice to cling to when no other guidance or clarity was to be found. "You serve and trust me to provide."

A little more insight would have helped. Maybe a follow-up memo or a heavenly heads-up that said something like, "Don't worry—in three months I'll lead you to the perfect opportunity. You're going to love it. It'll be exactly what you need. Just hold on."

But no. I didn't get any of that. Just silence. And in that silence, it became easy to start questioning not just God's nearness, but His love, His attentiveness, even His care. And maybe more subtly, I started questioning myself.

Was it my fault?

Was I the reason I couldn't hear?

Had I somehow blocked His voice?

None of this is new. In fact, it seems to be one of God's go-to moves in Scripture. Silence is often how He speaks. "Is the Lord among us or not?" That was the cry of the Israelites in Exodus 17, after the wilderness thirst set in and answers seemed nowhere to be found.

After losing everything, Job sat in the ashes, crying out to God with raw, honest questions. And for chapter after chapter, God said nothing. Job wrestled, doubted, lamented, and begged for a response. But the heavens stayed quiet. It wasn't until the very end of the book that God finally spoke—and even then, He didn't give Job the answers he wanted.

Even Jesus, in the Garden of Gethsemane, cried out in desperation—and we don't know if He heard a definitive "no" or nothing at all. But what we do know is that in that silence, He found resolve. Somehow, He still knew what His Father was saying. And maybe that's the kind of knowing I'm trying to learn, too.

Somewhere along the way, we all have to face that same question. And the harder the season, the louder the silence becomes. It doesn't just stretch—it settles in. It starts to feel like a weight. Like something pressing on your chest when you pray or hanging in the air when you open your Bible. But if we're paying attention, we start to hear echoes—faint and familiar—of others who've walked this same path. People who reached the end of themselves, sat down under the weight of it all, and begged God to just say something.

Mountaintop to Meltdown

Confidence can be a killer. On Mount Carmel, Elijah had swagger. The kind of boldness that comes from knowing—absolutely knowing—that God is with you. That your Dad can beat up their dad. He didn't just call down fire from heaven. He taunted the prophets of Baal while he waited. *"Shout louder!"* he said. *"…Maybe [your god] is deep in thought, or busy, or traveling. Maybe he is sleeping and must be awakened"* (1 Kings 18:27).

The English translations kinda "chicken out" on this. In Hebrew, it's a little more descriptive: "Maybe your god is relieving himself." Elijah was brazen. Full of fire—both literally and figuratively. You can almost see him, like Kobe in a Game 7—pure Mamba mentality. Locked in. No hesitation. Absolutely sure he could hit the game-winning shot.

Elijah rebuilt the altar, dug a trench around it, poured water all over the wood. Once. Twice. Three times. Until everything was soaked. And then he prayed—not a long, showy speech, but a simple plea: "Let it be known today that you are God in Israel…and that I am your servant."

And God answered. Fire fell from heaven and consumed the offering, the wood, the stones, the soil—even the water in the trench. Mic drop.

The people collapsed in fear and awe, crying out, "The Lord—He is God! The Lord—He is God!"

They disposed of the prophets of Baal—all 450 of them—and then, as if to tie a bow on the entire display, Elijah told King Ahab, "Go eat and drink, for there is the sound of a heavy rain."

Elijah climbed to the top of Mount Carmel, bowed low with his face between his knees, and prayed for rain. At first—nothing. But then, on the seventh time, his servant spotted it: a small cloud rising from the sea, no bigger than a man's hand. That was enough. Elijah stood up, and Ahab rode off to Jezreel.

It wasn't just a weather forecast. It was prophecy fulfilled. Israel had been in severe drought for more than three years—a judgment Elijah himself had declared. And now, after fire from heaven and a national turning point, came the final confirmation: *rain*.

Mercy, after judgment. Provision, after famine.

It's the kind of spiritual high that most of us dream about. Bold faith, divine fire, public vindication, prophetic victory. And then…rain. It was everything a prophet could ask for. Everything a believer might hope God would do when they step out in trust. And yet, just a few verses later, Elijah is unraveling.

Jezebel heard what happened and vowed to kill him. And the same man who stood alone on the mountain ran alone into the wilderness. The confidence had gone, and the silence had settled in.

Elijah collapsed under a broom tree and prayed, "I have had enough, Lord…Take my life" (1 Kings 19:4).

It's a dark place when you'd prefer death over life. When you go from the mountaintop to the valley. From mocking false gods to questioning if the true God is even listening. But that's the thing about wilderness: It doesn't matter how confident you were yesterday. Even the strongest moments can evaporate in the heat of today.

Mercifully, God didn't rebuke Elijah for his collapse. He didn't tell him to toughen up or get over it. He simply let him rest. He sent an angel to touch him gently, twice, and told him to eat.

Bread. Water. Sleep. Sometimes the most spiritual thing God gives is a nap and a meal. Only after that did Elijah begin the long, slow journey to Mount Horeb—the mountain of God.

There, hidden in a cave, God asked a simple question: "What are you doing here, Elijah?"

In Scripture—and in life—God's questions are never for His benefit. He's not gathering information. His questions are always invitations. They peel back layers. They press on wounds. They stir reflection. When God asked, *"Where are you?"* in the garden, or *"Who told you that you were naked?"* (Genesis 3), He wasn't looking for directions or facts. He was inviting Adam into self-awareness, into confession, into intimacy.

And here, with Elijah, it's no different. God was inviting him to name what's really going on—not the prophet-mask version, not the tough exterior, but the truth inside his chest.

Elijah answered with honesty: "I have been very zealous for the Lord…[but] I am the only one left, and now they are trying to kill me too" (v. 14).

It's raw and a little whiny…but it's real. And that's what God was after. He didn't call Elijah to the mountain to give him a lecture. He called him there to let him unravel in His presence. Sometimes the most important thing God does in the wilderness is ask the kind of question that allows us to finally say what we're really carrying. And then, in His own tender and patient way, He reminds us of who He is—just like He did with Elijah.

"Go out and stand on the mountain in the presence of the Lord" (v. 11). A windstorm came—violent enough to shatter rocks. But God wasn't in the wind.

Then an earthquake. But God wasn't in the earthquake.

Then a fire. But God wasn't in the fire.

And then…a gentle whisper. A still, small voice.

That's where God was.

Not in the power display. Not in the noise. Not even in the kind of dramatic response Elijah had known before. This time, the voice came low. Quiet. Subtle. And yet, unmistakably holy.

This story matters because it reframes everything we *think* we know about how God speaks. Elijah knew what it was like to hear from God in big, unmistakable ways.

He had seen fire fall.

He had watched the heavens respond to his prayers.

He had heard God speak with clarity and conviction.

And still—even this prophet of God had to learn how to recognize the whisper. But it took a collapse of everything Elijah expected from God—a full burnout moment—to clear the static and give him the ears to hear.

Oftentimes, that's what we need, too.

The Loudest Silence

It's funny how the wilderness screams when God seems silent. It's a strange and exhausting paradox. The external chaos, the inner noise, the nonstop swirl of questions and fears—it all feels deafening. And yet, God's voice? Crickets. Or at least, that's how it feels.

The silence becomes sharper because everything else is so loud. Pain has a volume. So does confusion. So does loss. As Nigel Tufnel famously said in *Spinal Tap*, "These go to eleven." (Google it.) And when everything in your life feels uncertain, the noise does, too—it goes to eleven.

Sometimes it's the noise around us—emails that never stop, headlines that never rest, bills piling up, kids melting down, group chats buzzing with opinions, and a culture that runs on outrage and urgency.

Other times, it's the noise within us—unresolved thoughts, buried emotions, fears we can't name, and the quiet pressure to hold it all together. We carry a storm in our chest, and it drowns out the stillness we once could hear.

We live in a noisy world—and we carry noisy hearts. Our pace, our feeds, our to-do lists, our habits of distraction. They shape how we relate to God. We're conditioned to expect quick answers, constant stimulation, and immediate relief. So when God doesn't speak on our timeline, we don't just feel disappointed—we feel disoriented. If He's not loud, we assume He's not there. If He's quiet, we assume we've done something wrong.

But what if the problem isn't just the silence—but how we respond to it? Because the truth is, we often don't know whose voice we're listening to. We second-guess. We spin in circles. One moment we think it's God; the next, we wonder if it's just our own anxiety or imagination.

We trick ourselves. We overthink. We replay old lies. And without clear direction, we start to doubt even what we once knew to be true. In the absence of clarity, we start to reach for certainty anywhere we can find it—even if it's not from God.

And it's not just our own thoughts we wrestle with. Those voices around us start to chirp, too—friends, family, pastors, podcasts. Everyone has an opinion. Everyone has advice. Everyone wants to help you "fix it," "get better," "move on."

Job's friends did the same thing. So did his wife. They all had ideas about why he was suffering and what he should do about it. But none of them truly understood what God was doing in the silence. Sometimes the hardest part of silence isn't just what you're not hearing from God—it's what you are hearing from everyone else.

There's a deep temptation to expect God's voice to be loud and obvious. After all the fire and fury of Mount Carmel, Elijah ran straight into the wilderness—expecting, maybe even needing, God to speak the same way again. But what he got was silence. No voice. No answer. Just exhaustion. He was undone. He thought God's presence would look like it did before—loud, powerful, unmistakable.

But God wasn't in the wind, or the earthquake, or the fire. He was in the whisper. And Elijah had to relearn how to hear Him there.

We want the same things Elijah wanted: the fire from heaven, the billboard, the breakthrough. And yes, sometimes God does speak that way. But more often—if Scripture is any indication—He doesn't. More often, He speaks through stillness. Through Scripture. Through the quiet conviction of the Spirit. Through community. Through seemingly ordinary moments that we almost miss.

So why does God seem silent in our most desperate moments? If He knows we're struggling—if He sees our pain—why does He hold back? Why doesn't He break through?

There's no easy answer. But silence, I'm learning again, is not absence. Silence is how God forms us. He strips away the noise not to punish us, but to invite us deeper. He removes what we've been leaning on—our formulas, our expectations, our comforts—so we can lean on Him instead. And in that silence, something shifts.

Silence has a way of peeling back the polished version of ourselves. The version we try to present to God and to others. When we stop performing, when there's no emotional high to carry us, when all that's left is the ache—we get honest. We say things like, "I'm done." "I'm tired." "Where are you?" "Do you even care?" And those aren't signs of failure. They're signs of intimacy. Signs that the pretense is gone and something real is happening beneath the surface.

In the wilderness, platitudes don't really work. Pat answers tend to fall flat. No quote on a coffee mug can reach into the kind of ache that silence brings. What we need isn't a phrase—we need presence.

Silence may not mean something's wrong. It might mean something sacred is happening. Something slow. Something beneath the surface that can't be rushed. Sometimes silence is the work. It's God drawing us out. It's how He clears out space so we can actually hear. Not the voice we want, but the one we need.

No One Immune

"Please pray for me—the longing for God is terribly painful and yet the darkness is becoming greater. What contradiction there is in my soul. The pain of longing is so great—that I just long and long for God—and then it is that I feel He does not want me—He is not there—Heaven—souls—why these are just words—which mean nothing to me. My very being is not wanted by God."[2]

At first glance, these words sound like they came from someone uncertain in their faith—someone still learning how to trust God in the dark. They read like the kind of struggle we don't say out loud in church—the kind we secretly believe "mature" believers should've grown out of by now. The kind of weakness we're taught to hide behind forced smiles and well-rehearsed faith statements.

Maybe you think they were written by someone new to faith. Or a whiny Gen X'er like me. But I didn't write those words. They came from Mother Teresa, recorded in her personal journals and later compiled into the book *Come Be My Light*. Yes, that Mother Teresa—the saint in the streets of Calcutta. The woman whose name is synonymous with selfless love and boundless compassion. She was a spiritual giant in the eyes of the world. But deep inside, she was locked in an invisible battle, haunted by silence, and worn thin by the enemy's lies.

After experiencing a vivid and personal calling from Jesus in 1946 to leave her convent and serve "the poorest of the poor," Mother Teresa stepped into the streets of Calcutta with a heart on fire. She described hearing the voice of Christ so clearly—an intimate sense of His presence, love, and calling. In her letters, she called it "the Voice," and it came with tenderness, urgency, and unmistakable clarity.

Jesus had asked her to be His light in the darkness, His hands for the forgotten, His love for the unloved. And she said yes. Without hesitation. She left the comfort of the convent and walked into the chaos of poverty, sickness, and death. She clothed the naked, fed the hungry, and cradled the dying. But not long after that radical obedience—after she gave everything—something shifted. The Voice that had once spoken so clearly went silent. The nearness she had known disappeared. All of it vanished.

---

[2] Teresa of Calcutta. 2007. *Come Be My Light: The Private Writings of the "Saint of Calcutta."* Edited by Brian Kolodiejchuk. New York: Doubleday. p.210

She expected that following Jesus would be costly. What she didn't expect was that it would feel so alone. Within just a few years of beginning her ministry, she began writing letters to her spiritual superiors—begging for understanding, asking if something was wrong with her, wondering if she had offended God. The presence she once felt so deeply was gone, and all that remained was silence.

Cold. Prolonged. Unrelenting.

And in that silence, the enemy crept in. Not with temptation to abandon the mission. Not with rebellion. But with something far more subtle—and more dangerous. Lies. Lies that sounded like her own voice. Lies that told her she was unwanted. That she had been abandoned. That she had mistaken her calling. That heaven was empty. That her love meant nothing. In another letter, she wrote:

"There is so much contradiction in my soul—such deep longing for God—so deep that it is painful—a suffering continual—and yet not wanted by God—repulsed—empty—no faith—no love—no zeal... Heaven means nothing—to me it looks like an empty place."[3]

This wasn't a result of rebellion or a crisis of morality. It was a targeted spiritual assault, a slow and calculated distortion of what was true. In the midst of being a light to the darkest places, the enemy met her with lies meant to unravel her from the inside out. And yet—she kept going. She kept giving her life away, even while feeling like God had taken His away from her.

It may surprise you to learn that spiritual maturity doesn't make us immune to attack; it makes us a target. The Bible and history are filled with examples.

No one is immune. Not the faithful. Not the selfless. Not even the sainted.

No matter how much good we do, how much we sacrifice, how fully we give ourselves away—an active enemy has been given rule over this wilderness life, hates us with relentless passion, and stands in bold, unflinching opposition to all that is good, true, and holy.

---

[3] Teresa of Calcutta. 2007. *Come Be My Light: The Private Writings of the "Saint of Calcutta."* Edited by Brian Kolodiejchuk. New York: Doubleday. p.288

The enemy doesn't wait for us to be strong. He doesn't wait for the right time. In fact, he doesn't wait at all. His assault is relentless. He watches for the cracks—then forces them open. He moves in when we're vulnerable, unsure, and barely hanging on. He comes when we're tired. When we're disoriented. When we're asking questions we never imagined we'd ask:

Does God really care?

Is He even listening?

Why does this feel so hard—especially when I'm trying to do everything right?

He knows how to time his attacks. He is a master of accusation and temptation. And it's not just when we're careless or rebellious. It's when we're hungry. When we're sorrowful. When we're weary. And strangely—perhaps even strategically—he often targets those who are most deeply invested in the work of God. Because why wouldn't he? If you were out to diminish light, wouldn't you start with those holding the brightest flames?

His voice doesn't always sound evil. It often sounds familiar. Almost like our own thoughts. That's what makes it so dangerous.

It doesn't yell. It blends. It wraps itself in our weariness, our anxiety, our wounds…just enough to feel like truth.

Two Voices in the Wilderness

But the voice of God? It's different. Even when it challenges us, it brings peace. Even when it convicts, it draws us closer. Learning to tell the difference may be one of the most important disciplines of the spiritual life.

The enemy's voice accuses and condemns. God's voice convicts—with kindness and clarity.

The enemy creates panic and pressure, pushing and rushing. God's voice invites peace, even in pain.

The enemy isolates, convincing us that no one understands. But God always draws near—even when we try to run.

The enemy mocks, "You're not enough," and demands you prove your worth. God says, "You are mine," and invites you to rest.

If the voice you're hearing drives you deeper into fear, shame, striving, or isolation, it isn't Jesus. His voice may be firm, but it is never harsh. It may convict, but never condemn. God's voice leads to repentance. To restoration. To return. The enemy's voice pushes you into hiding.

In a world full of noise and a wilderness full of whispers, we must become people who listen carefully. Because the difference between condemnation and conviction isn't small. It's the difference between shame and healing. Between drifting and returning. Between defeat and resurrection.

This is how the enemy works: quietly, strategically, unrelentingly. He doesn't need to control your life. He just needs to bend your perspective. Just enough to make you question God's heart. Just enough to slowly, almost imperceptibly, pull you away from trust.

Spiritual warfare doesn't always look like fire and demons. Most often, it looks like discouragement. Cynicism. Numbness. Self-reliance. Isolation. It looks like a life that quietly stops expecting anything from God. Stops believing He's near. Stops trusting at all.

And in the wilderness, those questions don't echo in the abstract. They land deep. They shape how we see God and ourselves. How we respond. Because victory in the wilderness doesn't mean we avoid temptation. It means we learn to recognize the voice of the liar and choose to trust the voice of truth. Even when it's quiet. Even when it's hard. Even when it doesn't feel like enough.

That's the battle. Not out there. But in here: where spiritual war is often fought in silence. And trust is the loudest weapon we have.

Quiet That Won't Quit

Eventually, every one of us faces a fork in the road. When God seems silent—when prayers feel like they're bouncing off the ceiling—we have a choice: Will we walk away? Numb out? Distract ourselves and move on? Or will we lean in? Will we stay at the cave's edge, like Elijah, and wait for the whisper?

There are only two paths in silence: lean in or walk away. Silence will either close us off or open us up. We don't get to control how or when God speaks—but we do get to decide whether we'll stay close enough to hear it when He does. The wilderness does scream, especially when God seems silent. But maybe what seems like silence is actually an invitation. Maybe God is already speaking—just not in the way we expected.

And maybe the stillness isn't empty after all. Maybe it's holy ground inviting us to listen.

What we think is silence is often just subtlety. God hasn't left us—He's just not shouting. He's moving, speaking, leading…but not always in the format we expect. It's not that He's far away—it's that He's communicating at a frequency we're not used to tuning into.

In the wilderness, that kind of subtlety can feel like absence—especially when we're tired or afraid. But the longer I walk with Him, the more I'm learning: God's quiet doesn't mean He's disengaged. It means He's drawing us deeper. Teaching us to recognize His voice not just in the dramatic moments, but in the daily ones. In the ordinary. In the quiet that won't quit.

Elijah needed to learn how to recognize God—not just when He was undeniable, but when He was near. We do, too. Because more often than not, God still speaks through quiet things. Through a passage of Scripture that lands a little differently this time. Through a conversation with a friend who says something they didn't even realize you needed to hear. Through a closed door that makes space for something new. Through tears. Through beauty. Through silence itself.

It's not always obvious. That's why Jesus said, "My sheep listen to my voice; I know them, and they follow me" (John 10:27).

It takes familiarity to hear a whisper. It takes time. Stillness. Proximity. Learning the difference between God's voice and all the other ones. And the good news? You don't have to get it right every time. You just have to keep listening.

Because nothing in the wilderness is wasted. Not even the quiet. The things that feel small—mundane conversations, tired prayers, background music, passing thoughts—God can use any of it.

Often, it's the ordinary moments that become sacred ground. God isn't always obvious. But He's never far. As the psalmist said, "The Lord is close to the brokenhearted and saves those who are crushed in spirit" (Psalm 34:18). You may not feel Him. You may not hear Him. But He's close.

Learning to Listen

If you're wandering right now…if the silence hasn't lifted yet…if you've prayed, waited, and wondered why you haven't heard anything—take heart. You're not alone. And you're not broken. The goal isn't to figure it all out. It's to stay open. To keep listening. To stay close enough to hear when the whisper comes.

There's no formula, but there are ways we can posture ourselves to hear better. Just like tuning a radio or leaning in to catch a quiet voice across a noisy room, here are a few gentle rhythms that can help us become more attentive:

Immerse yourself in Scripture. If you want to know what God sounds like, start with what He's already said. The Bible isn't just an ancient text—it's a living voice. When everything else is unclear, His Word remains steady. You don't need to read a lot. Pray one psalm all week. Read one chapter each day or every other day. Let it marinate. Ask God to speak through what you're reading. And pay attention to what sticks with you throughout the day.

Create space for stillness. Silence doesn't just happen—you have to choose it. Turn off the music. Put the phone in another room. Sit quietly for ten minutes and do nothing. Don't pray, don't read, don't listen to anything. Just be still. At first, it will feel uncomfortable, maybe even pointless. But stillness is a discipline. The more you practice it, the more natural it becomes. And often, God speaks into the space you create, not the noise you provide.

Pay attention to where you sense His presence. Is it when you're walking? Driving? In the shower? When you're serving others? In creation? During worship? Does God speak to you through dreams? Where does His voice tend to resonate with you? That's something to notice and lean into.

Ask better questions. Instead of "Why aren't you speaking?" try "How are you speaking that I'm not recognizing?" Instead of "Where are you?" try "Where am I not looking?" God is likely moving—but maybe we're not paying attention.

Trust the community around you. God often speaks through other people. Through a friend's wisdom, a pastor's sermon, a conversation with a stranger. Don't dismiss the possibility that God is using someone else's voice to reach you. Be open to how He might speak through the others, and pay attention to whether what you're hearing is consistent with what you know about God from His Word.

Keep a record. Write down the ways you sense God's presence, even if they seem small. Not because you need to prove anything, but because remembering helps. When the next season of silence comes—and it probably will—you'll have evidence of His faithfulness to embrace.

As you practice these things, try not to fixate on what God isn't saying. Pay attention to what He has said. What He is doing. What has remained steady—even when everything else feels shaky. And above all, keep listening. Keep seeking. You don't need to chase clarity. Just stay near.

Sometimes God speaks through a whisper. Sometimes through His Word. Sometimes through silence that draws you deeper into trust. But always—always—with love. And when you're tired, discouraged, or unsure what comes next, take a cue from none other than Dory from *Finding Nemo*: Just keep swimming.

You don't need to have it all figured out. You don't need to see the shore. You just need to keep going. One act of trust at a time. One step closer. One breath, one prayer, one moment of faithfulness.

I've learned that silence and vulnerability make perfect targets. When we're stripped down, uncertain or reaching for God's voice in the quiet, other voices get louder. When we're tired from listening, disappointed from waiting or raw from wrestling, the whispers that aren't from God sound most convincing. The enemy knows our weak spots, and he knows exactly when we're most susceptible to lies that masquerade as truth.

Silence isn't just an invitation to hear God more clearly; it's also an opportunity for deception to slip in when our defenses are down. And if we're going to learn to recognize God's whisper, we'd better learn to recognize the voices that aren't His.

The wilderness teaches us to listen carefully. Because in the silence, both God and the enemy whisper. And learning to tell the difference might be the most important skill you develop in the wilderness.

II. Why the Wilderness

"I think things come into our lives to help us get from one place to a better one."

— *Ted Lasso, Season 1*

4. What in the Wilderness?!

Tracing Our Pain Back to the Source

> "We know that the whole creation has been groaning as in the pains of childbirth right up to the present time. Not only so, but we ourselves, who have the firstfruits of the Spirit, groan inwardly as we wait eagerly for our adoption to sonship, the redemption of our bodies" (Romans 8:22–23).

It All Hurts

A few years ago, during a routine physical, my doctor leaned back in his chair, smiled, and said, "Remember, while you're in your forties, you still have to go looking for trouble. In your fifties, trouble will start looking for you."

At the time, I shrugged it off. But now, having crested into my fifties, his prophetic word hits a little too close to home…pretty much daily. Turns out, the guy with the M.D. actually knows what he's talking about—and as you get older, groaning becomes a regular rhythm of life. These days, I groan when I get up out of a chair. I groan when I bend down to pet the dog. I groan—loudly—after playing volleyball with my 13-year-old daughter and her friends. It's like all my joints are filing a formal complaint against gravity itself.

One of my "favorite" moments? Throwing out my back while carrying a cardboard box. An empty cardboard box. I spent three days flat on my back, staring at the ceiling and wondering exactly when my body decided to turn against me. You young people may scoff…but it'll come for you, too.

I used to think groaning was reserved for the very old, the very injured, or the overly dramatic. Now I realize—it's part of life. Every creak, every ache, every oof is a reminder: My body is breaking down. And that's just the outside..

The wilderness catches up to all of us, just as aging does. When we're young, we assume we can outrun it. We believe, with just the right combination of hard work, faith, wisdom, and maybe a few lucky breaks, we can avoid the pain—or at least minimize it. But life has a way of proving otherwise.

Struggle and suffering don't discriminate. They don't care how much money you make or how often you show up to church. They don't check your resume, your background, or your theology. Pain finds pastors and addicts, moms and CEOs, introverts and influencers. It comes for the faithful and the skeptic, the disciplined and the self-destructive. And often, it sneaks up on us in more than one form.

Sure, sometimes we bring it on ourselves—we shoot ourselves in the foot with pride, bad decisions, or old wounds we've never dealt with. Other times, we find ourselves in the blast radius of someone else's sin, left picking up the pieces of what we didn't choose and can't control. And then there are the moments we can't explain, when tragedy shows up uninvited and leaves us breathless.

This isn't new. It's been happening for generations. The groaning of our world echoes through every headline, every diagnosis, every sleepless night.

Broken Down

The groaning we feel in our bones, our minds, our relationships, and even in the weather are all part of a world that's no longer as it should be.

The apostle Paul uses the Greek word for "groaning" (*stenazō*) in Romans 8:22 to represent a deep, guttural, wordless ache that is not merely a casual discomfort. Instead, it refers to the labor pains of childbirth …suffering that holds on to hope.

It's an ache we feel when we know how things were meant to be and yet feel the gap of what is. And it shows up everywhere.

Physical Groaning: Our Bodies Break Down

Paul makes it personal. "We groan inwardly," he says, "as we wait for… the redemption of our bodies." (And yes, that includes the back pain from the cardboard box.) Even our physical weariness points to the fall.

He then expands on this in 2 Corinthians 5:2–5:

"Meanwhile we groan, longing to be clothed instead with our heavenly dwelling…so that what is mortal may be swallowed up by life. Now the one who has fashioned us for this very purpose is God, who has given us the Spirit as a deposit, guaranteeing what is to come."

In other words, our groaning isn't aimless. It's directional. It's not the cry of despair but the ache of anticipation. Paul compares our current bodies to tents—temporary, fragile, vulnerable. And he describes our longing not as escapism, but as a deep desire for what we were always meant for: to be fully alive, fully whole, fully at home.

We weren't made to simply endure slow decay, but to experience eternal renewal. Not to be discarded, but to be transformed. Resurrection isn't an upgrade—it's a restoration. It's not about ditching this life; it's about God finishing what He started, redeeming even our physical selves. So when your back goes out or your knees ache, when the diagnosis comes, when you can't sleep or can't move like you used to—it's not just aging. It's a whisper that things are not yet as they should be.

But it's also a promise. The Spirit within you is a guarantee that one day, all of this groaning will be swallowed up by new life as it was meant to be.

Emotional Groaning: The Pain Inside

Groaning isn't always visible. Often, the loudest pain is the silent one. In Psalm 6:6, David wrote, "I am worn out from my groaning. All night long I flood my bed with weeping…" And in Psalm 32:3: *"When I kept silent, my bones wasted away through my groaning all day long."*

David knew deep anguish—both from the wounds inflicted on him and the wounds he inflicted on himself. He carried the weight of his own failures: adultery (some would say rape), deception, and murder. He hid his sin for a season, and the silence nearly crushed him. This is the inner groaning—anxiety that won't quiet, depression that hangs like fog, the exhaustion of carrying pain no one can see.

We live in a broken world where trauma leaves scars, where mental health struggles are real, where some days the weight of simply existing feels overwhelming. And this emotional groaning isn't a sign of weak faith—it's a sign of being human in a fractured world.

I think about stories like Chester Bennington—the former frontman for the rock band Linkin Park. Despite his money, fame, talent, and a massive fanbase, he carried such deep pain it eventually swallowed him whole. He once said in an interview, "This place right here, this is a bad neighborhood. I should not be in here alone." [4] He was pointing to his own mind. His honesty is haunting. It wasn't like he was unaware of his struggles, nor did he lack the resources to get help. Yet, it proved not to be enough, and he took his own life in July 2017.

It's not just true of him. It's true of so many of us. Our minds can be hard neighborhoods to live in. Our hearts can feel like deserts. And no amount of success or spiritual activity makes us immune to that reality.

This is the wilderness. And eventually, it finds us. The question isn't whether we'll suffer; it's what we'll do when the groaning begins.

Relational Groaning: Love That Hurts

Then there's the groaning that comes from being human with other humans. We were created for connection, but sin fractured our ability to love well. We wound the people we love most. We're disappointed by the people we trusted most. We carry generational pain—patterns of hurt passed down through families. We navigate the exhaustion of trying to repair what feels irreparably broken.

Even in the best relationships, there's a longing for something deeper, something more whole. We ache for the kind of love that doesn't disappoint, doesn't manipulate, doesn't abandon. The kind of love we were made for but can't seem to find—or give—consistently.

---

[4] Loudwire. 2017. "Chester Bennington Discusses Dark Thought That Inspired 'Heavy.'" July 21, 2017.

Still, Jesus said, "Love one another." Not because it's easy, but because it's necessary. Our relational groaning points us not only to what's wrong, but to the kind of community God is forming through grace, humility, and love. A people who reflect His nature—not just with words, but in the way we walk together through the wilderness.

Creation Groaning: The Earth Itself Cries Out

Finally, there's the groaning that surrounds us—the kind we see in headlines about hurricanes, fires, famine, floods, droughts, and disasters that leave entire communities shattered. We often call them "natural disasters," but Scripture offers a more honest framing: Creation itself is groaning. Like us, it longs for renewal. Every quake, every storm, every scorched field is a reminder that the world is not as it should be—that, as Paul wrote, all creation is in labor, waiting to be made new.

Creation is not just static background scenery in the biblical story. It's an active participant in both the tragedy of the fall and the hope of redemption. In Genesis 3:17–19, after Adam and Eve sinned, God declared that even the ground would be cursed because of them. What was once freely fruitful would now resist, bringing forth thorns and thistles. Work would become wearying. Survival would involve sweat and struggle. Even nature would bear the cost of humanity's rebellion.

Isaiah 24:4–5 reiterates this: "The earth dries up and withers…the earth is defiled by its people."

This is the biblical worldview: Creation bears scars not because it sinned, but because we did. It's been caught in the crossfire, impacted by humanity's pride, greed, exploitation, and violence. The land mourns. The waters rage. The skies hold back their rain or release it in floods. The very systems of the earth seem to cry out, "This isn't how it's supposed to be."

And yet, even here we find hope. Paul didn't describe the earth's groaning as the agony of death. He described it as "labor pains." It's not pointless suffering. It's pain with purpose. The earth isn't groaning in despair. It's groaning in anticipation, waiting—just like us—to be made new.

We feel this tension in our daily lives. We experience creation's beauty and brokenness in the same breath. A golden sunrise, followed by a wildfire. A gentle spring breeze, followed by a devastating tornado. A fruitful harvest, and a famine across the ocean.

The world still reflects God's glory, but it also echoes our fall. There's still awe. Still wonder. Still beauty that stuns us into worship.

But there's also groaning. A holy restlessness. Because just like us, creation knows it was made for something better. And just like us, it waits.

So we groan. In our bodies, in our minds, in our relationships, in our spirits, and in the very ground beneath our feet. But Scripture doesn't leave us in silence. It gives our groaning a voice. And more than that, it gives it meaning.

Fun at Parties

Hear me out—I'm not trying to be a "Debbie Downer" here. Life is still beautiful. The world is still full of wonder, creativity, and joy. But we can't ignore the foundational reality—both theologically and anecdotally—that brokenness runs through it all.

Genesis 3 tells the story of the first fracture. Adam and Eve, living in perfect harmony with God, with each other, and with creation, chose to trust their own judgment over God's word. They wanted to be like God—to know good and evil, to be the arbiters of truth. But instead of becoming more, they became far less than God intended.

Their eyes were opened, but not to glory—to shame. Their hearts swelled—not with wisdom, but with fear. In that moment, the perfect harmony of creation was fractured. Peace gave way to hiding. Trust gave way to suspicion. Unity gave way to blame. And the ripple effects of that choice are still with us. The groaning we feel is the echo of Eden undone. The world is not as it was meant to be. And deep down, we know it.

What had been effortless—walking with God, intimacy with one another, living in a world that provided—suddenly became strained, painful, and broken. The fracture rippled outward—from soul to soul, from soil to sky.

God said the ground would no longer yield its fruit easily; humankind would eat "through painful toil" (Genesis 3:17). He said childbirth would now be marked by pain (Genesis 3:16).

The womb became a place of pain. Work became exhausting. Family became complicated. Life itself became fragile. The world, once a garden of delight, began to groan under the weight of what was lost. The earth would now produce thorns and thistles. Hearts would now produce fear and suspicion. Lives would now bear wounds we were never meant to carry. The effects of sin seeped into everything—bodies, relationships, systems, nature itself.

What had been whole was now splintered. Harmony didn't just fade—it broke. And we've been living in the aftershocks ever since.

So yeah, we groan. Not just in our bodies, but in our souls when we ache for wholeness. We groan in our relationships when we can't seem to fix what's broken. We groan when we look at the world—the wars, the disasters, the injustice—and feel helpless against it. We are all waiting, aching for the restoration of all things. Longing for the day when the wilderness will end and the true Promised Land will finally come.

But until that days comes, this is the wilderness life: caught between the beauty of what was and the hope of what will be, groaning and longing for redemption.

If this is just how life works—if groaning is normal and the wilderness is expected—then why?

Why does the path to the Promised Land have to lead through such barren places?

Why can't love be simple, faith be straightforward, suffering be rare? These aren't rebellious questions—they're honest ones. And the deeper we go into the wilderness, the more urgent they become.

This Hurts Me More Than It Will Hurt You

If God is so loving, why does life hurt so much?

This is one of the oldest and deepest questions we ask. And it's not just theological—it's very personal. It's the question that haunts us in hospital rooms and empty bedrooms. It's the whisper behind unanswered prayers and broken dreams.

Why doesn't God step in more?

Why does He let this keep happening?

It's the tension underneath nearly every struggle we face. Why cancer? Why heartbreak? Why miscarriages and betrayal and generational trauma? Why depression that won't lift and prayers that go unanswered?

It's not a new question. It's ancient. Job asked it. The psalmists cried it. Jesus screamed it from the cross: *"My God, why have You forsaken me?"* And if you've ever found yourself asking the same—know that you're not faithless. You're human.

Much ink has been spilled trying to understand and explain suffering throughout human history—and truthfully, we're probably not any closer to answers than we were 2,000 years ago. In the Bible, we're given some explanations that hold weight:

- We live in a broken world—fractured by sin, poisoned by pride.
- Paul says creation itself is groaning—longing for redemption.
- We have an enemy who loves to distort and destroy.
- As humans, we have free will—and we often use it to hurt each other.
- And we ourselves are bent inward, riddled with wounds and blind spots.

All of these reasons may be true, but when the suffering is deep—when it's your child, your body, your loss—those answers can feel hollow. They might be theologically correct, but they're not always comforting. You don't just want a reason. You want rescue. Especially when there's no one to blame—no obvious sin, no dramatic rebellion. Just loss. Just pain.

That's part of what makes the book of Job so uncomfortable. An entire book of the Bible is dedicated to one man's suffering and how utterly unfair it seems. Job lost everything—his wealth, his health, his children—and the people around him tried to explain it.

"You must've done something wrong," they said. "God must be teaching you a lesson." They tried to apply formulas. But Job knew better. He knew he hadn't done anything to deserve this. And when he cried out to God for an answer, for justice, for something to make sense of the pain…God spoke. But He didn't answer "why." He didn't sit Job down and say, "Here's what happened. Here's the reason."

Instead, He offered Job something we're often not prepared to receive: a reminder of who God is.

For most of us, that's frustrating. We want a reason so we can guard against it happening again. We want a why so we can convince ourselves the pain was worth it. We want to believe that life works on some kind of scale, where good behavior results in blessing and bad behavior results in consequences.

But it doesn't always work like that.

The world is broken in ways we can't fully fix (though we try—oh, how we try). And we are broken in ways we can't always see. And that's when we have to zoom out. Because maybe the better question isn't, "Why is life so hard?" Maybe it's, "Where are we really?"

We're not in Eden anymore. And we're not yet in the Promised Land. We're in the wilderness. The space where pain is real, but formation is possible. The space where we walk by faith, not by sight. Where comfort is fleeting but God is near.

And if this is where we live, the real question becomes: What is God doing here?

He's preparing us. The wilderness isn't punishment—it's preparation. Hebrews 12 offers us a different framework: "Endure hardship as discipline; God is treating you as his children…" (v. 7).

At first glance, that verse feels sharp—like a spiritual slap on the wrist. But let's pause for a second and think. It doesn't say all hardship *is* discipline. It says to endure it *as if* it were.

In other words, what if we received our pain not as punishment—but as something God could use to help us? Something formative? Something—dare I say—*loving*? That doesn't mean every hardship is God's doing. It's not.

Some pain comes from our own choices. Some from the brokenness of others. Some happens because the world itself is messed up. But the writer of Hebrews invites us to see it differently. Even in the pain, God is not absent. He's not indifferent. He's not punishing you (Jesus took our punishment). He's doing what a good parent does: shaping, forming, refining us.

But it doesn't feel like love, does it? Discipline rarely does.

Free Range

I was what you could call a "free-range" kid—the kind who came home to an empty house because Mom was working full-time to keep us afloat. By middle school, she had to leave for work by 7 a.m. and wouldn't get home until after 6 p.m. That meant I had a lot of freedom—and not the kind that builds character. If you've ever spent time around 13-year-old boys, you know they should absolutely not be in charge of themselves. I was no exception.

We lived across the street from my middle school, which made things very convenient. I had full access to all the comforts of home during the school day: a stocked pantry, a TV with cable, a couch with no attendance policy, and absolutely no adult supervision. Why settle for the cafeteria when you can have mac and cheese in your own kitchen? Why endure seventh period when your living room is showing "G.I. Joe"?

Needless to say, some friends and I started jumping the fence and "going home for lunch," which quickly turned into binge-watching our favorite TV shows for the rest of the day. We called it lunch. The school called it truancy.

Turns out, schools keep records of what classes you attend and don't. When my report card came out (which I intercepted before my mom saw it), there was quite a discrepancy in my attendance records. *Not a problem*, my underdeveloped 13-year-old brain thought. *I'll just forge one that has the right absences—and I'll polish up my grades a bit.* Unfortunately, my forgery skills weren't as strong as I thought, and I ended up caught by my mom—red pen-handed. In her frustration, she grabbed a belt to spank me with.

What I lacked in intelligence at the time, I made up for in agility—I managed to juke her direct attack, leaving the belt to simply wrap around my waist and fall to the ground. I couldn't help myself—I laughed. It was an out-of-body experience.

I could feel myself trying to grab the chuckle and pull it back as I watched her face go from hot with anger to cold with something far worse: resolve. She didn't grab for the belt again. She didn't have to. Instead, she calmly walked away and proceeded to methodically remove every shred of freedom I had left.

Skateboard? Gone. TV? Off limits. Friends? Not a chance. I was lucky to still have breath in my lungs. And just to really drive the lesson home, she actually turned me and one of my friends into the school and asked them to give us detention—the rat—which they gladly did.

Looking back now, I can't blame her—and honestly, I don't know how she held it together as well as she did. She did the best she could with what she had to work with. And as a parent myself now, I can say with full conviction: Discipline is complicated. There's this constant internal debate: Where do you draw the line? When do you extend grace, and when do you allow consequences to do their work? How do you correct without crushing? How do you guide without overcontrolling?

It's a balancing act that I still get wrong more than I'd like to admit. Because discipline isn't just about behavior—it's about formation. And that's what makes it so hard. You're not trying to punish your kid. You're trying to shape them. You're trying to teach them something deeper, something lasting.

But it's messy. And it's rarely clear at any given moment whether you're doing it "right."

Now imagine that kind of shaping—but not in the hands of a limited, overwhelmed parent doing their best. Imagine it in the hands of a perfect, all-knowing, all-loving God. A Father who doesn't guess. Who never second-guesses. Who sees everything—not just this moment, not just this mistake, but the entire story.

He sees how your childhood informed your instincts. He sees the lies you started believing before you even knew you were being shaped. He sees every injustice done to you, every fear you carry, every trauma tucked just beneath the surface. He knows what's forming you, what's wounding you, and what's holding you back—even the parts you're blind to.

And not only does He see you, He sees the billions of others whose lives intertwine with yours. He sees how your story affects theirs—and theirs, yours. He holds the complexity of creation in His hands—not just the people, but the systems, the seasons, the ripple effects that stretch across generations.

He's not guessing. He's not reacting out of impulse. He's not trying to "figure it out" as He goes. He is sovereign. He is wise. He is deeply, relentlessly loving. And when He disciplines—or allows hardship to shape us—it's never out of spite or exhaustion. It's not punishment. It's not payback. It's purpose.

Like a loving parent, God disciplines with eternity in mind, with perfect clarity, and with a heart that breaks for us even as He refines us. That's what Hebrews 12 invites us into when it says, "Endure hardship as discipline; God is treating you as His children."

It's a beautiful idea. Comforting, even—on paper. To know that God sees us as His beloved kids—and that even our hardest moments are not wasted but used for our formation—is powerful. But let's not pretend that makes it easier to live through. Because when the pain is real—when life unravels, when prayers go unanswered, when grief hits like a wave—we're not usually thinking, "Wow, what beautiful discipline this must be."

No, we're often wondering, *WTH* (heck)! We're wondering if He's angry, or absent, or just too busy with someone else's miracle.

If God is really that loving, then why does it still hurt so much?

Why does he allow us to go through these things?

Why does it feel like He's silent?

Why does this feel more like punishment than parenting?

The Book of James actually takes it a step further: "Consider it pure joy, my brothers and sisters, whenever you face trials of many kinds..." (James 1:2).

Joy? Really? That sounds ridiculous. (Please don't text this to a friend going through a hard time as an encouragement!) It's worth remembering who was writing. When James said this, he was not speaking from a place of comfort. He pastored a persecuted church. And church tradition tells us he was eventually martyred for his faith. His encouragement isn't theoretical—it's forged in suffering, rejection, and sacrifice. He wasn't offering cliché theology. He was offering hard-earned wisdom.

James isn't asking for joy instead of sorrow. He's not about pretending everything's okay. He's not about putting a shiny spiritual gloss over real grief. But unfortunately, that's exactly what many of us have been taught to do—especially in faith spaces.

When things get painful, we reach for spiritual language as a kind of emotional shortcut, trying to move past the ache instead of walking through it. That's called "spiritual bypassing"—a term first coined by psychologist John Welwood in the 1980s.[5] He noticed this tendency while working with Buddhist communities. They would use spiritual practices and beliefs to avoid dealing with unresolved emotional wounds, relational issues, and personal pain. Instead of facing grief, anger, or fear directly, people would "float above" their suffering in the name of enlightenment or inner peace. It looked holy—but it was actually avoidance.

And now, decades later, I believe spiritual bypassing has taken deep root in modern Christianity, too. We may not be quoting Zen proverbs, but we're doing the same thing—just with a Bible verse attached. We slap Romans 8:28 on someone's tragedy like a Band-Aid. We say things like, "God's got a plan," or, "Everything happens for a reason" when someone's heart is breaking in front of us. We over-spiritualize and under-feel. We quote scripture like armor to deflect our actual feelings. We numb ourselves with Christian clichés instead of letting God meet us in the feelings and frustrations.

But that's not James's approach. He isn't asking us to put on a brave face and call the pain a blessing. He's inviting us to look deeper—to trust that even in sorrow, even in hardship, there is something being formed in us that can't be formed any other way.

This is the difference between bypassing and lamenting. Bypassing skips the pain to get to the promise. Lament goes through the pain with honesty, with trembling, with trust. It dares to say, "This hurts, and I don't understand…but I'm still here."

---

[5] John Welwood, *Toward a Psychology of Awakening: Buddhism, Psychotherapy, and the Path of Personal and Spiritual Transformation* (Boston: Shambhala, 2000).

That's the kind of faith James is calling us toward—not cheerful detachment, but rooted resilience. A faith that refuses to bypass suffering and instead looks for God within it.

Learning to Lament

Lament isn't wallowing. It's refusing to go silent. It's grief that still speaks to God. The Psalms are full of it—honest cries, raw questions, emotional unedited-ness: *How long, O Lord? Why have You forsaken me? My God, are You listening?*

These are survival prayers. And they turn toward God, not away from Him. They lift up their eyes.

That's the power of lament: It keeps the relationship intact, even when everything else is falling apart. The prophet in Lamentations 3 says it plainly: "I remember my affliction and my wandering, the bitterness and the gall… my soul is downcast within me" (v. 19-20). He's not minimizing what hurts—he's naming it.

But right in the middle of that honesty, he adds: "Yet this I call to mind and therefore I have hope: Because of the Lord's great love we are not consumed, for his compassions never fail" (v. 21-22).

He holds grief and hope in the same breath. And that's what we are invited to do, too. This is the heart of seeing beauty in the wilderness—not avoiding grief, but noticing God within it.

There is a moment in Jesus' story that lives right inside this same tension. Gethsemane. The garden where grief and glory collided. We tend to think of the cross as the place of ultimate sacrifice—and it is.

But Gethsemane was the place of surrender. The place of wrestling. The place where love chose to stay, even in the pain.

Alone in the shadows of olive trees, Jesus fell to His knees, overcome with sorrow. He said his soul was "overwhelmed with sorrow to the point of death" (Matthew 26:38).

He wasn't shrinking back from the cross physically—He was holding the weight of cosmic isolation, injustice, and coming separation from the Father.

With trembling words He prayed, *"Father, if there is any other way…"*

This was not weakness. It was love refusing to pretend. He named it. He felt it. He carried it in His body. And even then—even there—He surrendered: "Not My will, but Yours." Because His love was deeper than the pain.

Was this where Jesus "learned obedience" (Hebrews 5:8) through what He suffered?

Just sit with that.

The perfect Son of God didn't bypass the process. He learned something through suffering. We're not told exactly what—there's no list of growth milestones from the wilderness or Gethsemane. But that mystery makes it even more powerful.

Jesus wasn't disobedient. He didn't need correction. And yet, somehow, suffering formed Him into our sympathetic High Priest—one who suffers *with* us, not just *for* us. Was it there He learned to surrender in weakness? To resist escape when the cross was in sight? To say, "Not My will, but Yours," through clenched teeth and bloodied sweat?

We don't know. But we know this: He didn't skip the furnace. And if He needed suffering to shape His obedience, why would we think we don't?

We tend to treat pain as a detour—proof we've gone off course. But even Jesus walked the hard road, and it wasn't failure. It was formation. He was made perfect through suffering (Hebrews 2:10). Not morally—He already was—but made complete. Ready.

And maybe that's what God is doing in us, too. Making us whole through what we never would've chosen. So why assume we'll be formed without it?

But suffering doesn't just shape us—it reveals us. It exposes what's beneath the surface. Not to shame us, but to strengthen what remains. That kind of revelation—refined in fire—is more precious than gold.

This is the mystery we're invited to hold: The reality that grief and grace, sorrow and beauty, can occupy the same space.

Love Doesn't Quit

When I look back on that middle-school moment with my mom, I see something now I didn't understand then. She was trying to shape me. She was doing the best she could with what she had.

At thirteen, all I could see was control and consequence. But now, as a parent myself, I see what was underneath it: love. Frustrated love. Protective love. Love that didn't always get it right, but never gave up. And if that's true of a single mom just trying to keep her idiot kid in school and out of a juvenile detention center, how much more true is that of God?

Hebrews 12 helps us reframe the whole thing. "…Śe Lord disciplines the one He loves…[He's] treating you as His children" (12:6-7). This is not a distant deity throwing lightning bolts. This is *the* loving Father saying, "I'm still here. I haven't walked away. I'm with you in this, and I'm doing something in you and through it."

Yes, it still hurts. Yes, it still leaves marks. But as we talked about earlier: Even Jesus' scars remained after the resurrection. He could have come back without them—flawless, untouched. But He didn't.

Why? Because the scars told the story. They weren't shameful. They were sacred. A reminder that resurrection doesn't erase suffering—it redeems it. And our scars can do the same. They remind us not just of what we've endured, but of what has been formed in us through it. Of who we've become and who we are becoming. Of how God met us in the places we didn't think He would.

We don't naturally see suffering that way—nor do we want to. Especially in a culture that equates blessing with comfort, strength with self-sufficiency, and success with ease. But the Bible tells a different story. Over and over, God meets people in the wilderness—in caves, deserts, prisons, storms. Why? Because the wilderness strips away everything we think we need so we can finally discover the God we actually do. He doesn't cause every wound—but He never wastes one. As Henri Nouwen once wrote, *"Suffering invites us to place our hurts in larger hands."*[6]

---

[6] Nouwen, Henri J. M. 2004. *Turn My Mourning into Dancing: Finding Hope in*

That's what life in the wilderness ultimately asks of us: Not just to endure, but to entrust. To let go of our demand for explanation and control, and to place our pain in the hands of the One who is forming us, even when we can't feel it.

He leverages the full weight of this broken world—its sin, its sorrow, its sickness—to shape something in us that will last. He doesn't always fix it. But He always forms us through it. Romans 8 doesn't say all things are good. It says that "in all things God works for the good"—which means nothing is beyond redemption.

That's the invitation: To stop seeing the wilderness as a detour and start recognizing it as the path.

This isn't where we're stuck. It's where we're shaped.

What if God isn't trying to fix something around you, but rather form someone within you? He's refining you like silver—burning away what doesn't belong, even if it feels like you're being undone.

And He promises us that "His power is made perfect in weakness" (2 Corinthians 12:9). Not in our strength. Not in our certainty. Not in our performance. But in our weakness.

This isn't an easy hope. But it's real. And it's good. Really Good News. Because even in the wilderness—even in the uncertainty—God is here. He is working. He is forming. And He is not finished.

Hard Times. Nashville: Thomas Nelson, p. 11.

5. Cycles, Circles, and Self-Sabotage

Identifying the Patterns That Keep Us Stuck

"This is what the Sovereign Lord...says:
'In repentance and rest is your salvation, in quietness and trust is your strength,
but you would have none of it... Yet the Lord longs to be gracious to you;
therefore he will rise up to show you compassion'" (Isaiah 30:15,18).

What the Deuce?

Why toilet paper in a crisis? Can someone explain it to me? When the stock market crashes, when inflation spikes, when supply chains are compromised, when a global pandemic hits—the world collectively panics. And what do we do? We storm the grocery stores and clamor for the essentials. The one thing that will protect us and provide for us in the worst possible circumstances? Toilet paper. Not medicine. Not water. Not even canned beans or peanut butter. Toilet paper. I'm still not sure what we're prepping for! It's as if we all believe that crisis is a natural diuretic. If there is even a hint of a crisis, carts will overflow with multi-packs of Charmin Ultra Soft until shelves are bare, as if the true test of survival is how much two-ply we can stuff in our garage.

Now, I may not be maxing out my Costco membership on bathroom essentials, but I've done the same thing in other ways. I've clamored to control the uncontrollable. I've numbed fear with distraction. I've sprinted toward action instead of sitting with uncertainty. Because when a crisis hits—when life feels chaotic or fragile—doing something (even something dumb) feels safer than doing nothing. Panic needs an outlet.

And in the wilderness, the easiest outlet is often a poor response. I've tried to fix pain with planning. I've buried grief in productivity. I've fought spiritual dryness by binge-watching Netflix or scrolling endlessly through social media, hoping the noise would drown out the ache. Maybe you have, too. We all have our own version of "panic hoarding."

And it's not just global pandemics that reveal it. It's the job loss. The cancer diagnosis. The broken relationship. The long stretch of unanswered prayer. The season where God feels silent and the ground feels shaky. These are the wilderness moments, and they expose not just our pain, but our patterns.

The wilderness pokes at our deepest fears and reveals our worst reflexes. We don't wait well. We don't trust easily. We reach for what's closest, what's familiar, what makes us feel powerful—even if it has nothing to do with what we actually need. Most of the time, we're not even aware we're doing it. We just react. It's easy to laugh at a mountain of toilet paper. It's harder to admit how often we choose control over surrender, or activity over presence. But the truth is, we all do it. The wilderness exposes our compulsions and invites us to see them clearly—not to shame us, but to redirect us.

Beneath the absurdity is something painfully familiar. When the ground shifts beneath us—when life gets uncertain, fragile, or overwhelming—most of us don't instinctively slow down and trust. We react. We reach for whatever makes us feel safe, in control, or at least distracted. And when I step back and look at my own life, I realize this isn't a one-time thing. It's a pattern. And I'm not alone.

The truth is, this isn't a new struggle. We're not the first to panic, grasp, or try to take matters into our own hands when life unravels. In fact, this same pattern shows up time and again in Scripture. And this is part of what I love—and honestly, sometimes hate—about the Bible: It doesn't clean things up. It doesn't edit out the failures or spiritual meltdowns. It shows them in full detail. For every display of courageous faith, there are three moments of doubt, fear, complaining, blaming, or trying to take matters into our own hands. The Bible doesn't just tell us how to get it right; it shows us all the ways people got it wrong and how God responded anyway.

Life in the wilderness has always been a revealing place. It doesn't usually create our dysfunction—it exposes it. It draws out the places where trust is thin, where fear runs deep, and where we'd rather control than surrender. And it helps us see behind the behavior to the lies we believe:

God won't come through.

I'm alone in this.

If I don't fix it, it'll all fall apart.

The more I read these wilderness stories, the more I see myself—not just in the faithful, but in the forgetful, the frustrated, and the ones grasping for idols. The Bible is as much about negative examples as it is positive. It's not just a guide to what faith should look like. It's a mirror—showing us the shortcuts, the emotional reactions, the panic-fueled decisions, and the incredible patience of God amid it all.

So maybe the real invitation in the wilderness isn't to figure everything out. Maybe it's to notice what rises up in us when we don't have control—and, most importantly, to become aware of our reflexes and let God meet us right there.

The Cycle of Self-Sabotage

The story of Scripture is as much a masterclass in how not to follow God as it is a guide for walking with Him—especially when it comes to Israel. God's chosen people, called out of slavery and into covenant, spent more time disgruntled and defiant than trusting and obedient. They were a stiff-necked people, prone to wander.

But before we point fingers, we should slow down. Look closer. Be more honest. Because Israel's tendencies aren't ancient anomalies—they're uncomfortable reflections. We are far more like them than we care to admit.

If you study Israel's story closely, a pattern begins to emerge—a cycle that plays out repeatedly:

- A lack or threat arises (hunger, danger, delay).
- They respond with fear—grumbling, blaming, or taking control.

- God still provides—often miraculously.
- They disobey or forget, turning to idols or false saviors.
- God patiently disciplines them but remains present.
- Rinse and repeat.

Each time they chose the familiar over the faithful, each time running back to Egypt instead of trusting forward, the soil of their hearts grew a little harder. A little more prepared for compromise. What began as panic and ended in golden calves eventually led somewhere unthinkable.

Let's trace how the erosion happened—not just to observe them, but to see ourselves within them.

Shiny Objects (Exodus 32)

Remember when Moses was on the mountain with God? As the story goes, the Israelites felt abandoned. Their leader had been gone forty days and forty nights—longer than anyone expected. The silence became unbearable. Where was he? What was taking so long? Had something happened to him? Had God forgotten about them?

Their anxiety built until they couldn't stand it anymore. "Come," they said to Aaron, "make us gods who will go before us. As for this fellow Moses who brought us up out of Egypt, we don't know what has happened to him" (v. 1).

Notice the language: "this fellow Moses." The man who stood before Pharaoh, who called down plagues, who led them through the Red Sea. Suddenly, he was reduced to "this fellow," as if they barely knew him.

Fear has a way of rewriting history, diminishing the very people God has used to rescue us.

So the people gathered their gold—earrings, bracelets, jewelry—and forged a new god with their own hands. Not because they've forgotten Yahweh's name, but because they couldn't handle waiting anymore. They needed something visible. Tangible. Controllable. Something that wouldn't disappear up a mountain for weeks without explanation.

Aaron fashioned the gold into a calf, and they declared, "These are your gods, Israel, who brought you out of Egypt" (v. 4). Their fear rewrote their memory. Their panic hijacked their theology. Rather than acknowledge God for the miracles He had performed just months earlier, they gave credit to a piece of metal they had just built.

Then they built an altar and declared a festival. They were not abandoning worship—they were trying to control it. They wanted God on their terms, in their timing, in a form they could manage. The golden calf represented the ultimate human impulse: to have God without having to trust God.

We do this, too. When God seems slow, we react. When His timeline stretches beyond our comfort, when the silence goes on longer than we think it should, we take blessings and turn them into idols—careers, relationships, platforms, ministries, even our families—reshaping them into golden calves that give us the illusion of control. We pour our gold into them: our time, energy, identity, security, hope. We tell ourselves we're being responsible, strategic, wise. But really, we're just afraid God won't come through in time.

We make idols out of our work, believing that the next promotion or pay raise will finally give us the security God seems slow to provide. We make idols out of relationships, needing constant affirmation and reassurance, expecting people to heal wounds only God can touch. We make idols out of our image, carefully managing how others see us because their approval feels more immediate than God's acceptance. We make idols out of our children's success, our church's growth, our bank account's balance—anything that gives us a sense of control when God feels unpredictable.

Not because we've stopped believing entirely, but because we're afraid He won't come through in time. And somehow, we think we know better.

The golden calf wasn't about theology. It was about fear. And if we're honest, our golden calves usually are, too. We still believe in God—we just want backup plans. We still trust Him—we just need something tangible to hold onto while we wait. But our golden calves always demand more gold. And eventually, what we created to help us ends up enslaving us.

Meat Over Manna (Numbers 11)

God was providing daily, directly, miraculously. Manna each morning—dependable, gentle, nourishing. A quiet miracle. But over time, it became monotonous. "We remember the fish we ate in Egypt at no cost…" (v. 5).

At no cost? Were they forgetting that Egypt had been the place of whips and oppression and genocide? But now, in the wilderness, all they could remember were the flavors. The spice of slavery. Their memory had been edited by discomfort.

So they grumbled. Their complaints grew louder. They demanded meat, displaying both ingratitude and distrust in God's provision. So God told Moses He would give them meat—not just for a day or two, but for an entire month: "…tntil it comes out of your nostrils and you loathe it" (v. 20).

Then God caused a wind to drive quail in from the sea. The birds covered the camp in massive piles, stretching in every direction, about three feet deep. People gathered obsessively—some collected thousands of pounds. But as they were still eating, before they could even swallow, God's anger burned. A severe plague broke out. Many died, not from hunger, but from the very abundance they demanded. The place became known as Kibroth Hattaavah—the "graves of craving."

Are we any different? We get bored with God's ordinary faithfulness. We want what others have—what looks more flavorful, more immediate. We romanticize our past dysfunctions when the present feels flat. We treat daily bread like it's a curse, not a gift. But God's provision isn't meant to entertain us—it's meant to form us.

When we demand more—when we grumble about God's timing, His methods, His pace—He sometimes gives us exactly what we ask for. Not because it's good for us, but because we refuse to trust Him. We get the job we demanded, the relationship we insisted on, the lifestyle we craved.

Just like Israel, we gather obsessively. We hoard. We consume. We think more will finally satisfy the ache inside. But abundance without gratitude becomes its own prison. What we thought would bring life starts to feel heavy, burdensome, even toxic. The very thing we demanded begins to destroy us—not because God is cruel, but because we chose our cravings over His character.

Every time we demand meat, we have to ask: Are we really hungry…or just restless? Are we seeking provision…or just running from the discomfort of trust?

Refusing the Promised Land (Numbers 13-14)

At the edge of promise, fear took over. Moses sent twelve spies to scout the Promised Land—the very land God had sworn to give them. They returned with evidence of God's goodness: grapes so large it took two men to carry a single cluster; pomegranates; figs. The land truly flowed with milk and honey, just as God promised.

But ten of the spies focus on something else entirely—the giants. "We saw the Nephilim there," they reported. "We seemed like grasshoppers in our own eyes, and we looked the same to them" (13:33).

Fear distorted their identity. They forgot they were God's chosen people. They forgot He had never failed them. They forgot the plagues in Egypt, the parted sea, the defeated armies. Despite all God had done, they panicked. "We should choose a leader and go back to Egypt," they said (14:4).

Egypt again. They'd rather return to slavery than trust God with uncertainty.

When God invites us into uncertainty, we do the same thing. We crave guarantees. We want to see the whole staircase before we take the first step. We pray for breakthrough but resist the cost. We ask God to open doors but demand He show us exactly what's on the other side first.

When the giants come into view—relationally, financially, emotionally, vocationally—we focus on their size instead of God's faithfulness. We rehearse our inadequacies instead of remembering His track record. We convince ourselves that maybe going back wouldn't be so bad after all. Maybe the job we hated wasn't that terrible. Maybe that relationship was better than being alone. Maybe the comfortable dysfunction was safer than the risky unknown.

We choose the familiar chains over the uncertain freedom, forgetting that God has never brought us this far to abandon us now.

Judah's Alliance with Egypt (Isaiah 30)

Centuries later, the pattern deepened. Judah faced the growing Assyrian threat—a massive empire swallowing nations one by one. King Hezekiah and his advisors panicked. Instead of turning to the God who had delivered them countless times before, they secretly negotiated with Egypt—the same Egypt that had enslaved their ancestors for four hundred years, the same Egypt God had devastated with plagues, the same Egypt they had escaped through the parted Red Sea.

But fear made them forget. They drafted alliances, sent envoys loaded with tribute, made elaborate political plans—but they didn't pray. They strategized but didn't seek God. They acted but didn't trust.

Through Isaiah, God pleaded with them: "In repentance and rest is your salvation, in quietness and trust is your strength, but you would have none of it" (v. 15).

They couldn't sit still. They couldn't be quiet. The urge to do something—anything—felt more comfortable than waiting on God. But God saw their frantic activity for what it really was: a lack of faith dressed up as wisdom.

"Yet the Lord longs to be gracious to you;"therefore he will rise up to show you compassion," Isaiah told them (v. 18). God waited with longing, not folded arms. His heart broke as He watched them run to the very nation He delivered them from.

When pressure builds, we do the same thing. We form alliances with old coping mechanisms we swore we'd never use again. We make peace with idols that offer the illusion of stability. We reach for what's worked before, even if it once enslaved us. We go back to the job that crushed our soul because it feels safer than trusting God with our finances. We overeat because it brings comfort, we reopen destructive apps we'd deleted, we call people who need to be cut off for good. Egypt looks appealing when the giants seem too big and God seems too quiet. And all the while, God says: "Come back. Rest. Trust. I've got you."

Each time Israel chose Egypt over trust, something in their hearts calcified. Each compromise prepared the soil for the next. What began as fear-driven reactions eventually led somewhere unthinkable.

The pattern was set: When threatened, run to Egypt.

When uncertain, make plans but not prayers.

When afraid, trust anyone except the God who had never failed them.

Where Egypt Leads (Jeremiah 7; 2 Kings 23)

What began as grumbling and panic in the wilderness eventually grew into something horrific. After generations of compromise, spiritual drift, and running back to Egypt, Israel wasn't just dabbling in idolatry—they were immersed in it. They built high places to foreign gods on every hill and under every green tree. They set up Asherah poles. They worshiped the sun, moon, and stars. They consulted mediums and spiritists.

And then we read this chilling indictment: "They have built the high places of Topheth in the Valley of Ben Hinnom to burn their sons and daughters in the fire—something I did not command, nor did it enter my mind" (Jeremiah 7:31).

These were their own children. God's chosen people—created to bear God's image—were now destroying His image in the most literal way. The very ones set apart to be a light to the nations were offering their sons and daughters to Molech, a false god who demanded the ultimate sacrifice.

Parents walked their children into the fire, believing this would bring blessing, security, favor from the gods. This wasn't some sudden collapse into madness. It was the end result of a slow, corrosive erosion—a drift that began in the wilderness with fear, impatience, and running back to Egypt. Each compromise made the next one easier. Each time they chose control over trust, familiar over faithful, Egypt over God, their hearts grew harder and their vision dimmer.

And if we're paying attention, we see ourselves. Our idols may not be carved from stone, but when we keep running back to our own versions of Egypt—the comfort of busyness, the familiar numbness of screens, the illusion of control through overwork, the safety of image management—we end up offering our children up, too.

We sacrifice them to endless schedules that leave no room for rest or relationship. We offer them to absent presence—physically there but emotionally elsewhere…always checking phones, always distracted, always somewhere else. We give them lives shaped by unchecked ambition where worth is measured by performance and love feels conditional on achievement.

We model the pursuit of success and refer to it as "calling." We reward busyness and call it "faithfulness." We celebrate hustle and name it "stewardship." We teach them to optimize their schedules, maximize their potential, build their platforms, secure their futures—but rarely do we teach them how to wait, grieve, be still, and follow Jesus when it costs them something. We pass down anxiety as inheritance. We hand them a faith that looks more like survival than flourishing, more like performance than presence.

We don't mean to. Most of us don't realize we're doing it. We tell ourselves we're providing, protecting, preparing them for the real world. But in our striving, we raise a generation shaped more by anxiety than abiding, more by achievement than acceptance, more by what they do than who they are. The very children we're trying to protect end up paying the price for our inability to trust God with our own fears.

Know Your Enemy

Why does it seem that the wilderness exposes our worst patterns and reflexes? Because we're not just struggling with our own weakness. We're being targeted.

Satan isn't all that creative, but he is consistent. His tactics haven't changed much since the beginning. From the garden to the wilderness to the battlefield of our own minds, his goal is the same: Twist what God has said, distort who God is, and fracture our trust in the process.

In Genesis 3, the serpent's first move wasn't rebellion—it was distortion. "Did God really say…?" With that one question, he started unraveling Eve's trust in the goodness of God. He reframed God's command as restriction instead of protection. He convinced her the only way to get what she needed was to take it for herself. The lie wasn't that the fruit was evil—but that God was withholding something good. The whisper was clear: "God can't be trusted. You're better off on your own." And the whisper worked.

Centuries later, Jesus found Himself in a different kind of wilderness—forty days of fasting, silence, and solitude. He was weak, hungry, alone. And the enemy showed up again with the same strategy. "If you are the Son of God…"

The challenge wasn't just about power; it was about identity. The temptations were painfully familiar: Turn stones to bread (self-reliance), throw yourself down and force God's hand (testing God's love), bow down and skip the pain (shortcut to glory).

It was Genesis all over again. But Jesus didn't waver. He didn't grasp. He didn't panic. He spoke truth. He trusted. Where Eve doubted and took, Jesus trusted and waited.

The enemy knows how to time his attacks. He is a master of subtlety and accusation. And he doesn't just go after careless rebels. He targets those who are most deeply invested in the work of God. Because if you wanted to diminish light, wouldn't you start with those carrying the brightest flames?

And when he comes, he doesn't just attack circumstances—he distorts perspective. The wilderness already disorients us. It bends what's real. Makes us vulnerable. Confuses our sense of who we are and what's true. And in that vulnerable space—when the hunger is real, the grief is sharp, the silence stretches longer than we expected—the enemy speaks. Not always with screams; often with whispers. Not always with lies we'd easily spot; often with distortions close enough to truth that we start to believe them.

Two Voices in the Wilderness

The enemy's voice rarely sounds evil. Often it sounds familiar—like our own thoughts. That's what makes it so effective. It blends in. It wraps itself in our exhaustion, our anxiety, our disappointment. It speaks in half-truths with just enough credibility to sound convincing.

Satan accuses. He pushes with pressure and panic. He isolates, convincing us no one understands. He whispers, "You're not enough," and demands proof.

This is how the enemy works: quietly, strategically, unrelentingly. He doesn't need to control your life—just bend your perspective. Just enough to make you question God's heart. Just enough to pull you, slowly and subtly, away from trust.

But God's voice? It's different. God convicts rather than accuses. God invites with peace rather than pushing with panic. God always moves toward us and points us toward one another even when we try to run. God says, "You are mine," and invites rest rather than demanding proof. Even when it challenges us, it brings peace. Even when it convicts, it draws us closer. And learning to tell the difference may be one of the most important disciplines in the spiritual life.

If the voice you're hearing drives you deeper into fear, shame, striving, or isolation—it isn't Jesus. His voice may be firm, but it is never harsh. He may wound to heal, but never to destroy. God's voice leads to repentance, restoration, and return. The enemy's voice leads to hiding.

Spiritual warfare doesn't usually look like fire and demons. Most often, it looks like discouragement. Cynicism. Numbness. Self-reliance. Isolation. It looks like a life that quietly stops expecting anything from God. That stops listening. That stops hoping. That settles for survival.

And in the wilderness, those whispers don't echo in the abstract. They land. They shape how we see God, how we see ourselves, how we respond. Because the battle isn't just around us—it's in us. The real war is over trust. The real weapon is stillness.

Seeing the Signs

So how do we break the cycles? It starts with recognizing we're in one. We've seen Israel grumble, panic, build idols, and beg for escape. We do the same. Wilderness living exposes what's beneath the surface—the lies we've believed, the fears we've buried, the compulsions we've baptized. Most of the time, we don't navigate it well. We rarely pause to ask why we're doing what we're doing. We don't reflect—we react. But what if the first step starts with simply noticing it?

One of the most overlooked markers of spiritual maturity is emotional intelligence, the ability to name what's actually happening beneath the surface. Without it, we confuse drivenness for devotion and reaction for faith. We don't just need more effort—we need more *awareness*. Because God isn't just after our activity—He's after our honesty.

He wants the *real* us. The motive behind the ministry. The insecurity behind the control. The grief behind the bitterness. Transformation never begins at the surface. It starts underground. And if you want to grow something new, you have to dig.

But self-awareness alone isn't enough. We're not just battling our own patterns—we're being targeted. Satan's goal is to twist our legitimate struggles into destructive patterns. He takes our real pain and whispers lies about God's character. He amplifies our genuine fears into panic. He turns our honest questions into accusations against God's goodness.

Learning to tell the difference matters. When thoughts consistently drive you toward isolation, despair, self-hatred, or distrust of God—that's not just your weakness talking. When the voice sounds more like an accuser than a loving Father, when it demands proof instead of inviting trust—you're in a spiritual battle, not just an emotional one.

So before you reach for the next strategy, the next plan, the next golden calf—pause. Ask yourself what you're really feeling and what you're really fearing. What do you believe God isn't doing? And does this voice draw you toward God and others, or away from them?

Personally, I've found journaling helps get things out of my head and into reality. When I journal, I ask myself a few simple questions to prompt self-examination as I pray:

- What am I thankful for?
- What am I worried or thinking about?
- What am I longing for?
- What am I feeling?
- What am I excited about?
- Where do I want to grow?

They may seem obvious, but these questions have been significant in helping me ground myself, become aware of my inner life, and discern who I'm listening to.

Reflecting on questions like these aren't designed to foster shame. They invite honesty and can lead us toward wholeness. Because you can't repent from what you won't name. And you can't heal what you won't touch.

The wilderness doesn't just reveal your pain. It reveals your patterns. And God isn't shocked by either. He already sees it all—and stays.

He Just Can't Quit Us

In all our stupidity, disobedience, toddler-like temper tantrums, willful blindness to how we shoot ourselves in the foot—God stays.

He stayed faithful to Israel, He stays faithful to us…and not begrudgingly. The wilderness exposes us, but it doesn't repel Him. We assume He'll meet us once we've calmed down, cleaned up, repented, and gotten it right. But that's not how the story goes.

Israel grumbled, panicked, built idols—and still the cloud didn't lift. The fire didn't fade. The manna still came. The water still flowed. Their shoes didn't wear out. Grace, somehow, still covered the desert floor. His presence didn't wait for their perfection. It met them in their panic.

That's what's so staggering: Israel got it wrong more than they got it right—and God didn't walk away. His voice still spoke. His mercy still invited. His provision still appeared, day after day. The wilderness revealed their weakness—but it also revealed His character. His steadiness. His unshakable compassion.

Isaiah painted it clearly: This is the God who "longs to be gracious," who "rises up to show you compassion" (Isaiah 30:18). Not because we've earned it. Not because we've improved. But because that's who He is.

And what does He ask in return? Not productivity. Not performance. Not a spiritual to-do list.

Stillness.

"In repentance and rest is your salvation, in quietness and trust is your strength…" (Isaiah 30:15). But like Israel, we often "would have none of it."

We manage. We fix. We scramble for outcomes. And all the while, God is saying: Stop. Return. Rest. Trust Me.

Here's where we have a choice. God doesn't force us to reframe our patterns—He invites us to. The wilderness surfaces our reflexes, but we get to decide what we do with them. We can keep reacting, keep running to Egypt, keep burying our motives under spiritual language. Or we can pause. We can ask why. We can bring our real fears into the light and let God meet us there.

Stillness isn't passivity. It's not apathy. It's faith. It's choosing to stay when everything in you wants to run. It's listening when all you want to do is solve. It's receiving instead of controlling. Stillness anchors us—not because the wilderness becomes easy, but because we begin to see we're not alone in it.

David understood this. Hunted, betrayed, misunderstood—he knew the wilderness well. But instead of building strategies to save himself, he turned to presence.

In Psalm 63, while hiding in the desert, he remembered God's sanctuary. He clung to past encounters of glory when nothing around him felt secure. He declared, "…your love is better than life" (v. 3)—not because it felt true in the moment, but because he believed it was still true in the dark. He worshiped not out of denial, but as defiance—refusing to let despair win. David didn't wait to meet God on the other side of the valley. He encountered Him in it.

Maybe you've cycled through every default setting: The busyness that masks your discontentment. The blame that deflects your pain. The scrolling that dulls your soul. The spiritual language that hides your doubts. The problem-solving that won't sit still. The quiet resignation that feels safer than hope. And maybe you're still here—in the valley, in the unknown.

But what if the invitation isn't to escape? What if it's to reframe what you're seeing? What if God isn't waiting at the finish line, but sitting beside you now? What if the silence you feel isn't distance, but intimacy—an invitation to lean in closer?

This isn't where you expected to find Him. But here He is—steady in the silence, faithful in the tension, patient in your wrestling. Not waiting for the wilderness to end. Just waiting for you to see that He never left.

Israel shows us nearly every poor response imaginable: reacting with fear, blaming leaders, resisting surrender, building idols, chasing comfort, begging to go back. We follow the same map. We do what they did. And often, we do it with Bible verses and leadership language attached.

But we're not just battling our own weakness—we're being targeted. The enemy knows our vulnerabilities and whispers lies that sound like our own thoughts, amplifying our fears and distorting our perspective of God's character. The wilderness doesn't just reveal our patterns; it becomes the battlefield where those patterns are either reinforced by deception or transformed by truth.

But the point here isn't to leave us in despair. It's to tell the truth. Because truth is the first step toward freedom. And when we begin to tell the truth—about our fears, our failures, our hunger for something more—we begin to notice what's been there all along: grace in the grit. Beauty in the barrenness. Flickers of life even in the places that feel most broken.

God is not surprised by our failures. He doesn't flinch at our compulsions. The Scriptures call Him "long-suffering" for a reason. His patience is not passive—it's fierce. It waits. It invites. It celebrates every trembling step toward Him.

Think of a child learning to walk. The falls aren't failures. They're formation. Parents don't rebuke the stumbles—they cheer for the steps. That's what God does with us in the wilderness. He's not measuring our perfection. He's watching for our trust. He's not tallying our missteps. He's cheering every time we stop, return, and rest in Him.

So if you're feeling like you've blown it, hear this: God hasn't left. He's not done. He's not disappointed that you fell. He's delighted that you're still trying to walk. The invitation is simple but not easy: instead of reacting, choose to reflect. Instead of burying your motives, bring them into the light. Instead of running to Egypt, run to Him. You don't have to get it perfect. You just have to stop running long enough to let Him hold you up.

That's how to journey through the wilderness: Don't walk it alone. Don't walk it in denial. Don't walk it pretending you're not afraid. Instead, walk slowly. Walk honestly. Walk aware of your patterns. Walk toward the Presence that refuses to walk away. Because He is here with you—not waiting for you to get it right, but welcoming you to see Him rightly.

And in that reframing, everything changes.

III. Walking the Wilderness

> "I can be changed by what happens to me.
> But I refuse to be reduced by it."
>
> — *Maya Angelou, Letter to My Daughter*

6. Faithful Is Fruitful

Measuring What Matters Most

"Therefore, since we are surrounded by such a great cloud of witnesses, let us throw off everything that hinders and the sin that so easily entangles. And let us run with perseverance the race marked out for us, fixing our eyes on Jesus, the pioneer and perfecter of faith…" (Hebrews 12:1–2)

Big Fat Failure

"Why are we hiring a failed church planter to help us move forward?"

That was the question. Said out loud. In a room full of people. I had just been introduced as a consultant brought in to help a church navigate some major challenges. I didn't know all the dynamics yet, but I could tell there was tension. And there it was. The question that wasn't really a question at all (passive aggressive much?). It was a condescending shot across the bow.

The room fell quiet. A few people shifted in their chairs. There were some nervous glances, but no one stepped in. I did my best to respond graciously—and then the meeting moved on.

But I didn't. I sat there with the question hanging in the back of my throat—not because I needed clarification, but because I knew exactly what they meant.

A few years earlier, my family and I had poured everything—time, energy, emotion, prayer—into planting a church that no longer existed. It started with vision and momentum, anchored by a committed core group of families who believed in something new. But it ended with hard decisions, quiet grief, and the slow death of a dream.

During the pandemic, we chose to dissolve the church—not because we didn't care about it, but because we cared about the people more. After four years of sacrificial investment, our team was exhausted. Starting over from scratch felt like it would do more harm than good. We believed that helping people flourish outside that structure was more faithful than forcing something that was already breaking under the weight of burnout. And yet none of that made the label sting any less. Failed!

From the outside, I get it. A church plant that dissolves gets quietly filed under "didn't work." And there were parts of it that didn't. But something in me still resisted the word "failed." Because even as everything unraveled, something deeper was being formed in all of us who were part of it—endurance, humility, a clearer sense of who we were and who we weren't. We may not have built something that lasted in the way people usually measure success, but I was not the same man who started that journey. The people involved were shaped more into the image of Christ. Our community was impacted with the Gospel, and we were faithful to be who we were called to be, for as long as we were called to be it.

That "question" and that moment stuck with me. Not because I hadn't already grieved the losses of that season, but because it peeled back something deeper: how we often define success. That kind of public judgment gets into your bones. It starts asking questions no one hears but you:

Am I just not built for this?

Did we just waste time and money?

What if everyone was wrong to believe in me?

But that's exactly where the deeper work begins. Because The Gospel doesn't erase those questions—it invites us to look at them differently. It meets us right at the point of disillusionment—when what we built didn't hold, when what we hoped for didn't happen, when what we tried to carry finally gave way. And it whispers: *This isn't the end of the story. This is where grace begins its best work.*

Falling Forward

That's the Gospel. Failing forward. Not because failure is good in itself or something to romanticize—but because God meets us in it. He steps into the wreckage, the regret, the what-could-have-beens and begins building something holy.

The story of redemption has never been about clean résumés or perfect track records. It's about what God can grow from dust—about freedom out of failure, purpose out of pain, resurrection coming through death …not around it.

From the very beginning, Scripture has shown us that the breaking point is often the turning point. That failure isn't a sign that God has left the story, but sometimes the clearest evidence that He's rewriting it. Over and over again, in both Scripture and real life, we see the same pattern: Failure isn't a detour to growth—it's the very soil where that growth begins. You don't have to look far to see it.

Michael Jordan—arguably the greatest to ever play the game—was cut from his high school varsity basketball team as a sophomore. The final spot went to a taller player named Leroy Smith. Jordan was devastated. But that rejection didn't defeat him—it formed him. He trained harder, woke up earlier, obsessed over his game. Years later, when he was inducted into the Basketball Hall of Fame, he invited Leroy Smith to attend—not out of spite, but because he understood that being passed over was part of the making. "It's a good thing I was cut," Jordan said. "Because it made me work even harder."[7] His legacy wasn't built in spite of that failure—it was built because of it.

By every worldly standard, Jesus was a failure. He didn't look like the Messiah people hoped for. They expected a king, a revolutionary, a military hero—someone to overthrow Rome and restore Israel's power. But Jesus didn't arrive with an army; he came with stories. He didn't ride a warhorse; He rode a borrowed donkey. He didn't claim a throne; He washed feet. Even His own family didn't know what to do with Him. At one point, they tried to take Him home, convinced He'd lost His mind.

---

[7] Michael Jordan, *I Can't Accept Not Trying: Michael Jordan on the Pursuit of Excellence* (San Francisco: HarperSanFrancisco, 1994), 16.

He wandered from village to village with no real home, sleeping in borrowed spaces and depending on the kindness of strangers. He didn't surround Himself with the influential or impressive. His closest followers were fishermen, tax collectors, zealots, and doubters—an unqualified, inconsistent, often confused group of misfits. And when the crowds did show up, He rarely capitalized on the moment.

Instead of leaning into popularity, He'd say something controversial or confusing that sent people walking away. He didn't cater to power. He didn't try to make Himself more palatable. He frustrated the religious establishment, unsettled His followers, and regularly withdrew when people wanted to elevate Him.

He spent most of His time with the wrong people: outsiders, sinners, the socially disqualified. He challenged the righteous, comforted the broken, and never seemed interested in pleasing the crowds. He was rejected by His own people, the very ones He came to save.

And when it all came crashing down, His friends fled. One denied Him. One betrayed Him. The rest disappeared. He was mocked by the religious elite, dismissed by political leaders, and ultimately tortured and executed in public—crucified like a criminal under the authority of an empire He never tried to overthrow. No palace. No title. No résumé we'd celebrate. Just a cross.

If someone like that showed up today, we probably wouldn't follow Him. Not because He lacked truth or authority, but because He didn't look the part. He didn't present Himself as a leader. He didn't play by the rules of influence. We'd question His judgment—wonder why He wasn't more strategic, why He didn't have a clearer plan or a better sense of how to grow something sustainable. We'd say He was squandering His potential, surrounding Himself with the wrong people, giving too much time to the fringe and not enough to the influential. We'd wonder why He wasn't maximizing His gifts. We'd critique His tone—too sharp in some moments, too vague in others. Too offensive to the insiders. Too gentle with the outsiders.

And we probably wouldn't attend His church. It would feel disorganized, underwhelming, unbranded. No signage. No systems. Just a man with a presence that was hard to explain and a message that made us uncomfortable and challenged our sensibilities. He didn't look like success. He epitomized obscurity. Someone wasting an opportunity. Some would say He was a failure.

But that's the paradox of the wilderness.

And maybe that's the point. What if success in the Kingdom of God looks nothing like success in the world? What if the scoreboard we've been taught to obsess over—numbers, growth, platform, acclaim—means very little to Jesus? What if the real markers of faithfulness are quieter, more obscure things: dependence, resilience, repentance, and joy that somehow persists even in suffering?

Faithfulness isn't perfect. It's not clean or linear. It doesn't always produce quick results or impressive returns. It's slow. Sometimes painfully slow. Because fruit doesn't grow in a rush. It grows through roots that go deep, through ground that's often dry and hard.

The growth might not always be visible, but it's real. And it matters. When we measure our lives by the extraordinary, we miss the sacred significance of the unseen. When we define success by worldly standards, we risk overlooking the very things Jesus values most. In His Kingdom, success looks like sacrifice. The greatest often look like they're losing. And the path of faithfulness rarely looks impressive. But it's still the path marked out for us. And we're not the first to walk it.

Faithful Failures?

Scripture doesn't polish its people. It doesn't dress them up for admiration or edit out their complexity. It tells the truth: the raw, unvarnished truth about weakness, failure, and the long, uneven road of trust.

Nowhere is that more evident than in Hebrews 11. This chapter is often referred to as the "Hall of Faith," but it reads less like a trophy case and more like a gallery of contradiction. It doesn't showcase spiritual all-stars whose lives were shining examples of victory. Instead, it holds together the stories of real people—broken, complicated, deeply human—who still chose to believe God. They aren't remembered because they got everything right. They're remembered because, in the middle of everything they got wrong, they didn't let go of trust.

Noah believed God when no one else did. He built an ark while the world mocked him, obeying instructions that didn't make sense in a culture that had no category for faith. And yet, his story doesn't conclude in triumph. It ends in a tent, with drunkenness and shame, exposed and fractured.

Rahab was a prostitute, an outsider in every imaginable way. By religious and cultural standards, she was disqualified from the start. But when the moment came, she risked everything to protect the spies. She believed that the God of Israel was real, and her faith became the hinge point of her legacy. She's not only named in Hebrews 11—she's listed in the genealogy of Jesus Himself.

Moses spoke with God as a man speaks with a friend. He stood barefoot before burning bushes, led people through parted seas, and climbed the mountain where the law was given. But even he didn't enter the Promised Land. A single moment of anger and disobedience kept him from seeing the fulfillment of what he carried for so long. His leadership was monumental, and yet his story remained incomplete.

David—the shepherd, the psalmist, the warrior king—was a man after God's own heart. But also a man who abused his power, took what wasn't his, and tried to cover it up with deception and blood. His story spiraled into brokenness. And yet, through honest repentance and enduring faith, God called him "a man after His own heart."

These heroes of the faith don't represent the clean arc of victory we're conditioned to admire. Their stories are marked by faithfulness laced with failure, by courage interwoven with compromise, by boldness shadowed by deep regret. And yet, in all of it, God calls them faithful. In all of it, He names them as witnesses.

And then, as if to make the point unmistakable, the writer of Hebrews turns to us:

"Therefore, since we are surrounded by such a great cloud of witnesses, let us throw off everything that hinders and the sin that so easily entangles. And let us run with perseverance the race marked out for us, fixing our eyes on Jesus, the pioneer and perfecter of faith" (Hebrews 12:1–2).

This is not a shift to a new idea. It's a continuation, a response to the stories that came before. The "great cloud of witnesses" comprises these very people: Noah, Rahab, Moses, David, and so many others. Men and women who didn't get it all right, who didn't see every promise fulfilled, who didn't always finish strong in the way we might define it. And yet they are the ones who cheer us on. Not because they were perfect, but because they kept going.

This is not a call to performance or achievement. It is a call to perseverance. Hebrews 12 invites us into something deeper than the pursuit of success. It urges us to run our own race—not with flawless execution, but with enduring trust. To let go of the weights that slow us down, release the sin that clings to us, and keep moving forward. Not by sight, but by faith.

These witnesses speak to us from the pages of Scripture and from the wilderness of their own lives. They remind us that faithfulness isn't about unbroken progress. It's about staying in the story. It's about continuing to trust when the outcome is uncertain. It's about showing up with your scars and doubts and saying, "I'm still here."

Jesus affirms this very truth in His teaching. In the parable of the talents in Matthew 25, the master returned and commended his servant—not for doubling his return or outperforming his peers—but for one simple thing: faithfulness. He said, "Well done, good and faithful servant" (v. 23). Not "successful." Not "exceptional." Just "faithful."

It's a reminder that in God's economy, faithfulness matters more than outcomes. What He honors is not productivity or polish—but perseverance. In the Kingdom of God, **faithfulness is fruitfulness**. Not because it always produces visible results, but because it reflects the character of the One who calls us. Because it mirrors His perseverance. Because it abides in His love. Because it endures.

Digging Under Disappointment

Faithfulness doesn't always feel fruitful. We hope it will. Maybe even assume it should. Deep down, many of us carry the quiet belief that if we're obedient—if we show up, do what God asks, remain faithful—then at some point, it will pay off. We expect to see progress. Impact. Some kind of confirmation that we're on the right path.

But life in the wilderness tells a different story. Sometimes we love well, serve sacrificially, pray earnestly, and still nothing seems to move. We offer ourselves fully, only to be met with silence, resistance, or slow unraveling. No matter how faithfully we obey, the outcome can still look more like loss than fruit.

There's a particular pain that comes not from rebellion or avoidance, but from doing exactly what God asked and still watching it fall apart. We did the listening. We sought wise counsel. We fasted. We prayed. We said yes with open hands. And yet, the result still looked like failure.

Sometimes we pray, seek the Lord, hear clearly, gather people, give ourselves fully to the work—and the church still closes four years later. Not because we weren't sincere. Not because we weren't obedient. But because even when the call is clear, the fruit isn't always visible.

What do you do with that kind of ending? What do you do when the outcome feels like it contradicts the calling?

This is where expectations become dangerous, especially the unspoken ones. Because whether we admit it or not, most of us don't enter into obedience with empty hands. We come with hope, with imagination, with a quiet outline of how things might go if we trust God and do what He asks. Sometimes we even call those expectations "faith." But they're really predictions. Assumptions. Projections of how we think God will act, and when.

We are often quick to examine the results. We can name what didn't go the way we thought it would. We can point to the closed door, the collapse, the silence. We are fluent in disappointment. But we rarely examine the expectations underneath.

And here's the truth: Every disappointment is built on an unmet expectation. It's not just what happened that hurts, but it's what we *expected* would happen.

That's why disappointment is so disorienting. It calls into question everything we believed going in. What did we assume faithfulness would produce? What did we believe obedience would secure? What did we quietly expect God would do in return for our trust?

Many of us—even without realizing it—approach life with a formula tucked into our hearts. If I obey, things will get better. If I serve, I'll see impact. If I follow God's voice, the path will make sense. But faithfulness is not a transaction. It's not a bargain we strike with God. It's not a strategy for success. And when our expectations are rooted in what we hope to get rather than who we're walking with, we set ourselves up for heartache.

Which means this moment—this space between obedience and disappointment—is an opportunity. Not to give up. But to go deeper. To ask harder questions. To examine not just what failed, but what we expected to happen in the first place. Because maybe part of the wilderness is learning to lay down not just our fears, but our expectations. To loosen our grip on outcomes. To rethink what success means. And to remember that in the Kingdom of God, success isn't measured by results. It's measured by remaining.

Jesus made this point unmistakably in John 15: "If you remain in Me, you will bear much fruit; apart from Me you can do nothing" (v. 5). Not less. *Nothing*. Fruitfulness, then, isn't the reward for effort—it's the result of remaining.

Not striving. Not achieving. Simply abiding.

But abiding rarely looks impressive. It's slow. Quiet. Hidden. Sometimes it means staying rooted when everything in you wants to uproot and run. Sometimes it means praying again—even when the last hundred prayers felt like they vanished into silence. Sometimes it means showing up—not because it's working, but because He's still worthy.

This is the deeper invitation of faithfulness—not to be effective, but to stay. To remain in Him even when everything else feels unresolved. And in that place, something begins to shift. When the fruit is unclear, our motives are revealed. When expectations go unmet, the illusions we've carried begin to surface. When our best efforts seem to fall flat, the questions deepen—not just, "Did it work?" but "Who am I becoming?"

This is where what we call failure often becomes the death of lesser dreams. Dreams that were more about recognition than transformation. More about control than communion. More about visible outcomes than faithful presence. That kind of death is painful. But it makes space for something truer to grow.

As Ruth Haley Barton wrote, *"Let the disappointment do its work"*[8] We must allow disappointment to strip away what doesn't hold, to dismantle the expectations that were quietly shaping our faith. Let it draw us back—not to what we hoped would happen, but to God Himself. Not because of what He produces, but because of who He is.

Even Jesus was not exempt from this pattern. After His baptism—after the sky split open and the Father declared, "This is My Son, whom I love; with Him I am well pleased" (Matthew 3:17)—He wasn't sent immediately into public ministry. He was led by the Spirit into the wilderness: into hunger, obscurity, silence, and struggle. Not because He had done something wrong, but because even perfect love leads us into desert places.

And what does that tell us about how God sees the wilderness? It tells us the wilderness is not punishment. It is the place where striving loses its grip and surrender takes root. Where false identities fall away. Where deeper roots grow—not in applause, but in silence.

So when you find yourself there—still showing up, still loving, still obeying—but seeing no fruit, hear this: You are not off track. You are not failing. You are not forgotten. **You are being formed.**

And though the ground may feel dry and the sky may feel silent, something sacred is happening beneath the surface. The fruit may not be visible yet. But the roots are deepening. And in God's time, in God's way, that will be enough.

Stripped Down and Still Striving

As we walk this wilderness life, it's easy to assume God is far off—distant, silent, perhaps even disappointed. We imagine Him standing at a safe distance—waiting for us to find our way back, arms crossed as He watches us stumble through the confusion. Somewhere deep down,

---

[8] McKelvey, Douglas Kaine. 2017. *Every Moment Holy, Volume I.* Franklin, TN: Rabbit Room Press. (Liturgy: "A Liturgy for the Death of a Dream.")

many of us fear that unless we handle this season the "right" way, God might pull away—or worse, leave us to figure it out on our own.

But that's not how Scripture tells the story. After listing a long line of saints in Hebrews 11—men and women who wandered, wrestled, and waited—the writer didn't tie it up with triumph. He didn't celebrate their achievements. Instead, he turned to us, the readers, and extended a quiet, persistent invitation. It wasn't a call to perform better; it was a call to remain faithful.

He wrote, "Since we are surrounded by such a great cloud of witnesses"—a crowd made up of imperfect, unfinished, often misunderstood people who trusted God in the dark. And in light of their lives, we are urged to do three things: to throw off everything that weighs us down, to run with perseverance the race marked out for us, and to fix our eyes on Jesus, the pioneer and perfecter of our faith. This is not a formula for escaping hardship. It's a framework for walking through it faithfully. And faithfulness, in the kingdom of God, is never wasted.

Throw It All Off

The writer didn't only speak of sin. He told us to release everything that weighed us down. Often, the heaviest burdens we carry aren't visible to anyone else. They are inward. Quiet. Assumptions we never questioned. Fears we've grown used to. Expectations we didn't even know we had.

Few things tangle up our spiritual pace more than the quiet expectations we carry about how life is supposed to unfold—about how God should respond or how faithfulness should feel. We assume our obedience will lead to clarity, that our surrender will unlock momentum, that our sacrifice will yield visible fruit. And when that doesn't happen, the ache goes deeper than disappointment—it begins to erode our trust.

Alongside those expectations, we carry pressure to perform, fear of failing again, comparison that whispers we're behind, and shame that tells us we're not enough. These burdens don't always look like sin, but they cling to us just the same, quietly exhausting our strength and slowly distorting our view of God.

To throw them off is not to deny the hurt or ignore the questions, but to release control over the stories we've written for ourselves and return to the one God is actually telling. It's an honest, ongoing surrender—laying down our assumptions, our timing, our imagined outcomes—and turning instead toward freedom. It's learning to say, "God, I trust You more than I trust my expectations."

Run With Perseverance

This is not a sprint. It isn't a burst of emotional momentum that carries you to breakthrough. The very word "perseverance" assumes struggle—it expects resistance, anticipates pain, and understands there will be moments when quitting feels like the only rational choice.

The race marked out for us is rarely direct. It winds through heartbreak, delays, silence, and landscapes we never planned to enter. There are seasons when every step feels like a slow crawl uphill, and nothing around us seems to be changing.

Perseverance doesn't dazzle. It doesn't trend or shout its way forward. More often, it looks like showing up when your faith feels thin, sitting in Scripture when the words feel hollow, forgiving someone again even when it still hurts, or praying one more time though the last prayer was met with silence. It is slow, sacred defiance—the quiet decision to stay rooted when everything in you wants to run.

And perseverance doesn't mean you won't feel discouraged. It doesn't mean you won't cry, question, or feel completely emptied out. It simply means those moments don't get the final word. You keep walking—not from strength, but from grace. You show up again, carrying the ache without letting it carry you away.

In the end, this race isn't about speed, spiritual performance, or visible results. It's about staying in the story. Because in the Kingdom of God, the ones who finish well are rarely the ones who never wavered. They are the ones who stayed. The ones who limped forward. The ones who fell and got up again. The ones who fixed their eyes on Jesus when everything else was shaking.

Fix Your Eyes on Jesus

Jesus isn't a distant idea or a stained-glass figure; He's the one who has walked this path of struggle and suffering with perfect faithfulness—and who walks it still, beside you. He is not standing at the end of the wilderness waiting for you to get your act together. He's not measuring your output or silently grading your endurance. He is here, in the dust, in the weariness, in the quiet that lingers longer than you'd like.

He is not shaken by your confusion. He is not impatient with your questions. He is steady, present, and near. He has known this path intimately. He has been misunderstood and betrayed, abandoned by those He loved most. He has wept from exhaustion. He has prayed unanswered prayers. He has carried the full weight of grief and kept walking anyway. And when the cost was highest, He didn't run. He stayed.

This is the One we are privileged to look to—not only as our example, but as our companion and strength. He is the pioneer of our faith—the one who carved this road with His own suffering. And He is the perfecter—the One who finishes what we cannot, who carries us when our knees buckle and we forget why we started.

To fix our eyes on Jesus is not to ignore the pain—it is to choose where we look while walking through it. It is to remember that endurance is not about feeling strong, but about trusting the One who is. It is to let our vision be shaped not by outcomes or timelines, but by the unchanging faithfulness of the One who still walks with us in the dust.

This is not spiritual escapism. It is not forced positivity. It is the re-centering of the soul on the only One who can sustain it. It is how we remember, even when nothing around us shifts, that we are not lost—because He is here. And He is enough.

The wilderness, then, is not proof that we've failed. It is not a sign that God has pulled away. According to Hebrews, it is something else entirely: the discipline of love. Not punishment, but formation. Not rejection, but refinement. It is the sacred, intentional work of a Father who sees what we cannot, who walks with us not to break us down, but to build something in us that cannot be shaken.

This is not wrath. Jesus already bore that. What we carry now is the slow, merciful weight of transformation—the careful hands of God forming roots in us that run deeper than circumstances, deeper than outcomes, deeper than applause.

This is where fruit begins. Not in triumph. Not in speed. Not in clarity. But in perseverance. In trust. In showing up. In staying.

Because faithfulness is fruitfulness that reflects the heart of God. Not because it guarantees success, but because it forms something eternal.

So when the road feels long and your strength feels small, when the finish line disappears from view and the prayers seem to hang unanswered in the sky, remember what anchors you. Not certainty. Not performance. Not resolution. But Jesus.

And even when the landscape doesn't change, even when the silence remains, He stays. And that will always be enough to keep going.

It Ain't Over

If you've walked through this chapter with a sense of conviction or maybe even grief—grief over what didn't grow, what didn't work, what didn't last—you're not alone. And maybe there's an invitation. Not to redefine your past, but to reframe your pursuit. Because what if your life was never meant to be measured by outcomes at all? What if God is not evaluating your impact, but sustaining your faith? What if your "success" is not what you produce, but how you endure?

Isaiah 55:11 reminds us that His Word never returns empty. It always accomplishes something, even if we can't see it. Like rain that sinks into the earth or snow that softens the ground in winter, God's work is often slow, silent, and hidden. But it is never wasted. He sends it with purpose. He tends to it with patience. And in time, it brings forth life.

James 5 tells us to be patient like a farmer who tills the soil, scatters the seed, and then waits. Not passively, but hopefully. Expectantly. Because he knows something is happening below the surface. He doesn't dig it up to check. He trusts the process. And in the same way, we're invited to wait—not with clenched fists or frenzied effort, but with a quiet confidence that what God starts, He finishes.

You don't have to force fruit. You are not the vine. You are not the harvest. You are the branch. Your job is to remain, stay rooted when it would be easier to run and to keep showing up when nothing around you changes.

This is the invitation of the wilderness: Not to strive. But to surrender. Not to succeed. But to stay. So lay down the burden of needing to be impressive. Let go of the pressure to be productive. God is not looking for extraordinary outcomes—He is forming you into an enduring witness.

Because in the Kingdom of God, faithfulness is fruitfulness. It may not always looks like growth, but faithfulness always looks like Jesus. And He is the truest measure of a life well-lived. So root yourself again—not in what you see, but in who He is. And trust that this will be enough.

7. Don't Go Solo

The Wilderness Is A Group Project

"Let us hold unswervingly to the hope we profess…And let us consider how we may spur one another on toward love and good deeds, not giving up meeting together…but encouraging one another…" (Hebrews 10:23–25).

Silent Sin

It was the worst moment of my life.

There wasn't any yelling. No door slamming. No dramatic confrontation. Just silence. Me, lying on one side of the bed. My wife, lying on the other. Our backs turned. And the bed quietly shaking from her sobs. There was no denial. No defending. Just the sickening weight of reality settling in. I hadn't just disappointed her—I had wounded her. And I couldn't fix it. It's one thing to be caught. It's another to realize someone you love has been crushed by something you thought you could keep under control. That night exposed more than just a behavior. It exposed years of hiding, self-management, and silent shame I'd never dealt with.

Growing up, pornography was easily accessible in my home. It was so normalized, I didn't even think it was wrong. No one told me it could become a trap. It was just there. And in time it wasn't just there—it was part of me.

I had a chance to get help when I was fifteen. I had just become a Christian and was sitting in a small group of guys with our leader. One of my friends shared that he had been struggling with porn. Our small group leader lovingly challenged him and, at the same time, reminded him of God's grace. I remember the Spirit prompting me to share my own struggle. The door was open. It was a safe place. But I just sat there. I could've said something. I wanted to say something. But I stayed silent. Smiled. Nodded. We prayed for him, and I said nothing.

I often wonder what might have been different if I had told the truth that night. Instead, the cycle continued—for years. Struggle. Failure. Shame. Hide. Try harder. Fail again.

Rinse and repeat.

I told myself I could manage it. That it wasn't a big deal. That eventually I'd outgrow it, figure it out on my own, or that once I got married it would go away. But I didn't. I just got better at hiding. Better at lying. Better at pretending I was okay.

And the more "mature" I became in my faith, the harder it became to share honestly—because "mature" Christians don't struggle with these things. So I kept fighting on my own, like a game of Whac-A-Mole. I struggled to suppress it, discipline it, and convince myself that it would be fine. Until the night it wasn't.

I thought she was asleep. But she wasn't. She had walked in without me knowing. And in an instant, everything I'd worked so hard to hide was exposed. Years of struggle. Years of silence. Years of pretending.

What followed was heartbreak. For her, betrayal. For me, more shame. But as painful as that night was—and it was—the real tragedy started much earlier. Not in the act, but in the silence. In the choice I made, over and over again, to walk alone.

Looking back, I'm convinced the greatest failure wasn't the pornography. As damaging and painful as that was, the deeper issue was my pride and refusal to share—to let anyone walk with me. I was terrified of rejection. Ashamed of the truth. Too proud to be weak in front of others. And because of that, I had been walking alone in the wilderness, and I didn't have to.

If I had simply admitted my struggle earlier…opened up when I was fifteen in that small group…let someone see me earlier…there's a good chance I wouldn't have been lying in bed years later, unable to comfort the person I loved most because of the pain I'd caused.

I know I'm not the only one. Some of us isolate out of shame. Others out of pride. Some because a past wound taught us that people can't be trusted. Some because we're just tired—tired of trying to explain, tired of not being understood, tired of needing help.

Life in the wilderness feeds those lies. It quietly insists, "Don't burden anyone. Don't open up. You'll only make things worse." So we pull back. Numb out. All the while aching to be seen—and terrified of what might happen if we are.

But what if we weren't made to carry it all alone?

What if one of the greatest tragedies of the wilderness isn't the pain itself, but the loneliness we choose in response to it?

What if we could see the story differently—not as evidence that we're too broken for community, but as proof that isolation was never the answer?

I think of that night at times—how differently it might have gone if I'd simply risked being honest fifteen years earlier. Healing might have started sooner. Heartache could've been spared—not just for me, but for the people I love.

I didn't need someone to fix me. I needed someone to walk with me. And maybe that's what you need, too. Maybe you've been carrying something for a long time. Maybe you've been holding it in—hoping no one sees, praying it just goes away. Maybe it feels safer to keep your distance—to suffer quietly and call it strength.

Hebrews 10 speaks right into the tension we walk in. Not with spiritual pressure or shallow advice—but with a tender, defiant hope. It calls us to hold on to each other with hope and love. Even in the wilderness. Especially in the wilderness.

You Can Be My Wingman Anytime

There's an urgency in the words of Hebrews 10—like the writer knew how tempting it is to hide or let go when life gets hard. "Let us hold unswervingly to the hope we profess…" (v. 23). The pressure of pain, disappointment, and disillusionment wears us down. And when it does, we often drift. We isolate. We begin to believe that faith is something we have to hold on our own.

So the passage keeps going: "And let us consider how we may spur one another on toward love and good deeds…" (v. 24). That word "consider" isn't passive thinking. In Greek, it means to observe carefully and then act on what you see. It's an invitation to study the people around you and then do something about their needs. This isn't a solo command. It's a shared one—a call not just to endure, but to endure together.

This isn't just about church attendance. It's about being held. The command is clear: Don't give up meeting together. But the heart behind it runs even deeper: Hold on with hope. Love each other.

In this wilderness life, our instinct is to isolate. Pain turns us inward. Disappointment builds walls. And modern life makes it all too easy to disappear behind screens and schedules. Even the church has subtly bought into this cultural script—treating community like an event to attend rather than a people to belong to.

But what if we could challenge our instinct to isolate?

What if the very impulse to build walls was actually an invitation to tear them down?

Scripture tells a different story. From the very beginning, we were made for each other.

Genesis 2:18 says, "It is not good for the man to be alone." This happened before the fall—in Eden, in perfection, in full relationship with God. And still it wasn't enough. As the late Tim Keller points out, this is the first thing God calls "not good." [9]Adam didn't need more work or creation. He needed another person. Someone to walk with.

The fact is, our need for human connection isn't a product of the fall—it's part of the design. We are made in the image of a communal God—Father, Son, and Spirit—eternally united in love. To be human is to need others. To flourish is to be known, supported, and strengthened by community.

---

[9] Timothy Keller, "Marriage as Friendship," sermon on Genesis 2:18, Redeemer Presbyterian Church, New York, NY, preached September 2004. Available at Gospel in Life, https://gospelinlife.com (accessed September 30, 2025).

And yet, we live in an age of disconnection. Loneliness has become an epidemic. Depression and anxiety are on the rise. Suicide rates are climbing. We are digitally connected yet relationally starved.

But God, in His wisdom and grace, gave us a remedy: the church. Not a building, brand, or event. But a people, family, place to be known and to know. To carry and be carried.

The Christian life isn't a solo hike through this wilderness life. It's a shared pilgrimage, where we are surrounded by others who walk beside us, hold us up, and help us move forward when our legs give out. It doesn't rush. It slows down. It calls us to notice one another. To reflect on how our lives might help lift someone else. To ask what love looks like right now—for someone we actually see.

And the kind of encouragement this passage speaks of? It's not shallow affirmation or polite sentiment. The word "spur" (Greek: *paroxysmos*) is the same word used to describe sharp provocation—a kind of "holy agitation." There's force in it. Urgency. Not violence, but vitality. It's the kind of love that won't let someone settle into apathy. A wake-up call to keep the embers glowing. To be stirred into courage, not because we feel ready, but because someone believes with us and for us.

But you don't spur strangers. You spur people you've walked with—people you love enough to risk awkwardness and inconvenience. And that kind of presence becomes sacred, especially when life starts to unravel.

We see it all throughout Scripture. In Exodus 17, the Israelites were under attack. Moses climbed a hill with his arms raised in prayer. As long as his arms were lifted, Israel prevailed. As his strength faded and the sun beat down, Moses' muscles trembled. His hands dropped—and the enemy began to win.

That's when Aaron and Hur stepped in. Not to replace him. Not to lecture him. But to hold him up. One on each side. They found a stone for him to rest on. And then, with quiet faithfulness, they kept his arms raised until the battle was over. The victory didn't come from Moses' strength; it came from shared endurance.

We also see it in David and Jonathan. David, hunted and hiding, wondered if God had forgotten him. Jonathan found him in the wilderness—not to rescue, but to remind: "You're not alone." That's what real friendship does. It doesn't erase pain—it enters it.

And then there's Jesus. He could have done it all without human intervention. But He didn't. He invited His disciples into His life, His ministry, His prayers—even His grief. These weren't people who naturally belonged together. A tax collector. A zealot. Fishermen. Doubters. Failures.

Jesus didn't build a movement around similarity. He built it around shared direction. He walked with them, ate with them, wept with them. And in His darkest hour, He asked them to stay awake and pray—not because He needed assistance, but because He wanted their presence. Even Jesus didn't choose to suffer alone.

This is the kind of spiritual family the New Testament calls us into. Paul urged the church in Ephesians 4:3 to "make every effort to keep the unity of the Spirit through the bond of peace." That kind of language assumes difficulty. Unity doesn't come naturally. It isn't the path of least resistance. It requires grace, humility, and forgiveness.

And Paul didn't tell us to create it—he told us to *keep* it. The Spirit has already made us one in Christ. Our job is to protect what's already been given.

This unity isn't just about shared theology—it's about shared life. In 1 Thessalonians 2:8, Paul reflected, "Because we loved you so much, we were delighted to share with you not only the gospel of God but our lives as well." That's the heartbeat of gospel-shaped community. Not just sermons, but stories. Not just theology, but tears. Not just truth, but presence.

Throughout the New Testament, this pattern is echoed again and again—in the form of fifty-nine "one another" commands. Together, they form a kind of relational liturgy for how we walk through this wilderness life together:

Love one another.

Encourage one another.

Bear one another's burdens.

Serve one another.

Confess to one another.

Pray for one another.

You can't practice any of these in isolation. They only come alive when we stay, show up, and let each other in. Because in this wilderness life, we're not just trying to survive—we're empowered to thrive. We're trying to remember who God is, who we are, and how deeply we need each other.

You need people. They need you. And if we're going to thrive, we won't do it alone.

Staying at Arm's Length

We were made for each other. Scripture makes that clear. But living it out? That's where things get complicated. The deeper the struggle, the more we tend to isolate—becoming self-protective, suspicious, or just plain tired. Often, we feel like no one can truly understand what we're going through. But the wilderness was never meant to be endured alone.

We live in a world that's more connected than ever—and somehow, lonelier than ever, too. You can feel it under the surface. In the silence between texts. In the weight of scrolling through highlight reels while sitting alone in your apartment.

Recent studies say nearly eight in ten Gen Zers (79%) and seven in ten millennials (71%) report loneliness. We're more digitally tethered than ever…yet starving for real connection.[10]

And this includes all of us. We say we want community, but when it shows up inconvenient, awkward, or imperfect—we retreat. We chase meaningful connections through social media and texts; but in reality, it's counterfeit communication. It will never replace being physically present with someone.

---

[10] Cigna. Cigna U.S. Loneliness Index—2020 Report. Bloomfield, CT: Cigna, 2020. https://www.cigna.com/static/www-cigna-com/docs/about-us/newsroom/studies-and-reports/combatting-loneliness/cigna-us-loneliness-index-2020.pdf.

I think my neighbors are lovely people. They wave when they drive by. I'm pretty sure they go to church. But they have a cottonwood tree. And every May, I seriously consider putting their house on the market.

It starts small—just a few innocent-looking tufts floating through the air. Kinda whimsical, even. But within days, it's everywhere. My backyard looks like a blizzard hit. My pool turns into a cotton trap. My AC wheezes. My allergies riot. Every surface I just cleaned gets buried in fluff.

And it's not even my tree. It's theirs. Their yard. Their mess. But it keeps blowing into my life—my curated, peaceful, well-maintained little sanctuary.

I hate that tree. So much so that I once Googled: "how to poison a cottonwood tree without anyone noticing." (I'm probably on a government watchlist now.) I didn't go through with it. But I thought about it. More than once.

My relationship with this cottonwood feels a lot like life in community. We all want peace. But other people's stuff has a way of drifting over. Their trauma. Their drama. Their parenting. Their grief. Their theology. Their dysfunction. It doesn't stay contained. It floats. It clogs. It frustrates. It invades your calm.

Sometimes I don't want to carry anyone else's burdens. I have enough of my own. I'd rather just chop the tree down.

The wilderness doesn't give us that luxury, however. There's no relational bubble that stays untouched by other people's storms. We may build fences, but the fluff still finds a way through. Because this life—this wilderness life—isn't meant to be walked alone. The way forward is rarely clean. But it is always together.

What if the "fluff" that drifts into our lives isn't an invasion to resist, but an invitation to love?

Still, that doesn't make it easy. We hold people at arm's length then wonder why no one sees us. We long for pursuit but make ourselves unreachable. We want care but won't risk being known. We build walls for protection then ache from loneliness. This is the paradox: self-protection that feels safer in the moment but leaves us emptier in the long run.

And then there's our pace of life. We pack our calendars with appointments and obligations, keeping just busy enough to avoid the quiet space where loneliness starts to speak. We say we're too busy—and maybe we are. But the truth is, we make time for the things we value most. And if we're honest, we often value comfort over connection. Control over community. Efficiency over empathy.

And the church? Often it doesn't feel much different. Maybe even worse. We can sit in rows, listen to sermons, attend small groups that prioritize discussion over connection—and still walk away without a single meaningful interaction. We talk about Scripture, but not about our lives. We say the right things, pray the right prayers, and leave just as unseen as when we arrived.

We long for community but settle for content. We crave closeness but default to independence. We want depth, but we're afraid of being exposed. So we hold people at arm's length—all the while wondering why no one really sees us, pursues us, or cares.

But genuine relationships are always messy and inefficient. They require time we don't think we have, emotional presence we're afraid to give, and grace we sometimes don't want to extend. Without them, we live guarded, disconnected, and spiritually malnourished.

The Next Right Thing

To cultivate authentic community, we have to confront the ways we hold people at arm's length. It requires intentionality—choosing to aggressively and relentlessly prioritize relationships, embrace vulnerability, and create spaces where people can be truly known. It's about shifting from attendance to engagement, from information to transformation.

My childhood pastor talked often about doing "the next right thing." Sweeping changes can be overwhelming, but taking one step is not as difficult. So what should you do to establish authentic, God-given relationships?

Start by praying. Before anything else—pray. Ask God to guide you. To soften your heart. To give you boldness. Ask Him to set up divine moments —those unexpected conversations, connections, and appoint-ments that only He can orchestrate.

This doesn't need to be formal or eloquent. Prayer doesn't inform God of something He doesn't already know. He's already aware of your loneliness, your longing, your fears about being rejected or misunderstood. But prayer does something in us. It reorients our hearts. It reminds us that we're not managing this alone.

Name what you need. First to yourself. Then to someone else. If you're going to pursue meaningful community, begin by naming what you're longing for. Not just "I want community." That's too broad. Be specific.

Maybe you want people who will ask how your soul is—not just how your week was. Maybe you're longing for others who are learning how to pray so you don't feel like the only one fumbling through it. Maybe you are looking for an active friend to walk with and talk about life's journey. Maybe you just want a space where you don't have to filter, where you can be fully honest and still fully loved.

Start there. Ask God to help you find clarity on what's really underneath the longing. Then, when the moment comes, be brave enough to say it out loud: "I've been wanting to grow in prayer but honestly don't know what I'm doing. Want to figure it out together?" Or "I'm looking for friendships that go deeper than surface stuff. Can we grab coffee and actually talk?" Or even just, "I need people who are okay with me not having it all together. Is that something you'd be open to?" When we risk vulnerability and name what we're actually longing for, it's magnetic—it often gives others permission to name their own longing too.

Lean in. Before you go searching for something new, look again at what's already in front of you. Sometimes the community we're praying for is already present—we've just never slowed down enough to see it. That guy at church you always chat with in the lobby. The mom who lingers after pickup at the preschool door. The coworker who actually wants to know about your weekend.

Before you start hunting for a new group, a new circle, or a new church, ask yourself: *Is there anyone already in my orbit who's quietly longing for the same kind of depth I'm craving?* If so, start there. Be the one who names it. Share your desire for deeper connection.

Most life-giving community doesn't happen in a program. It happens in living rooms. At playgrounds. On bleachers during soccer practice. Around half-clean kitchen tables. You don't need more events. You need more intention.

Start the conversation. If you're part of a church, don't wait on a sign-up sheet or a sermon series. Start the conversation yourself. Ask someone in leadership how you can move toward connection. Not just, "What groups are available?"—but a deeper question: "How can I step into the kind of relationships I'm longing for, and how might I help create that space for others, too?"

Go into the conversation prepared—not just with expectations, but with clarity. Know what you're hoping for. Be able to name it. And then find out where those kinds of connections are being cultivated in your church—or where they could be.

Start searching. If you're not currently connected to a local church, it's time to start looking—seriously. Not passively. Not with your arms crossed, waiting for the ideal place to find you. But with intention, humility, and a whole lot of prayer.

Know what you're actually looking for—and what matters most. You're not shopping for a service. You're seeking a spiritual family. And families aren't built in an hour on Sunday—they're formed through shared meals, honest conversations, and people who are willing to walk with you through real life.

Stay when it's awkward. Real community doesn't form in a week. It builds slowly, often unevenly, and almost always through someone's willingness to go first. The truth is, most people live relationally reactive. They wait to be invited or pursued. But if you're longing for something deeper, you can't wait for perfect conditions—you have to start anyway.

And yes, it's hard. There will be seasons when it feels like you're the only one carrying the weight. Like you're always the one texting first, planning the thing, keeping the conversation going. You'll wonder why no one else seems to try as hard, and the temptation will be to pull back.

But don't. Keep showing up. Keep initiating. Keep asking the second question. Keep being the one who follows up, who remembers, who reaches out again—even when it's met with silence.

Because community doesn't deepen through convenience. It deepens through consistency. Through quiet persistence. Through the decision to love people not just when it's easy or mutual, but when it costs you something. Over time, that kind of faithfulness forms something sturdy and sacred. Not dramatic. Not always noticed. But real.

It'll Never Be Perfect

These aren't formulas. There's no one-size-fits-all blueprint for building the kind of community our souls crave. But they're a starting point—a few bricks laid in faith toward something stronger, something real. Because in this wilderness life, we don't need perfect people or polished structures. We need faithful ones.

If you're holding out for the perfect church, let me save you some time—you won't find it. And if you do, the moment you start showing up, it won't be perfect anymore. Because churches aren't made of ideals. They're made of people. And people are messy. Broken. In process. Just like you. Just like me.

As imperfect as it all may be, something sacred begins to happen when we take these steps—when we name our need, when we reach out, when we stop waiting for perfect and start choosing presence. That's when we begin to see it: the slow, quiet ways God shows up. In the person who texts just to check in. In the friend who doesn't offer a fix, just sits beside you. In the couple who invites you to dinner when they know you've had a hard week.

Not everything will be resolved. Not every ache will disappear. But somewhere along the way, if you keep showing up, you may begin to see God again—right in the middle of it. Not through spectacle. Not through certainty. But through love that stays. Through presence that doesn't flinch. Through people who walk with you—even in the wilderness.

Becoming Ride or Die

Community is hard. We carry wounds. We feel disappointment. Sometimes the very places or people we hoped would bring connection only deepen the pain. And yet—even in all of that—God shows up. Not always in the way we expect. Not with flashing signs or sudden answers. But through people. Through presence. Through faithfulness.

Sometimes God shows up in the arms that lift ours when we're too tired to keep them raised. Sometimes He comes through a text we didn't expect, a meal we didn't ask for, a conversation that lingers long enough to break through the silence. Sometimes He reveals Himself in the quiet presence of someone who doesn't try to fix us, but just offers to listen.

We often look for God in the dramatic. The breakthrough. The moment everything shifts. But more often than not, He comes gently. Through the people who refuse to let us disappear.

This is what the early church understood. They didn't gather because they had it all together. They gathered because they didn't. Because they were just like us—struggling wanderers trying to hold each other up.

Hebrews 10:24-25 reminds us of this rhythm: "And let us consider how we may spur one another on toward love and good deeds, not giving up meeting together…but encouraging one another…"

They didn't gather to fix each other. They gathered to remind one another. To carry burdens. To enjoy each other's company. To hold hope unswervingly—not because it always felt strong, but because they refused to let go.

That's the invitation for us, too. Sometimes the most spiritual thing we can do is simply to show up. To be the Aaron or the Hur who lifts someone else's arms—or to let someone else be that for us. To let go of the pressure to have the right words and just be present.

In a world where people walk away so easily, presence is sacred.

In a world where people walk away so easily, presence is sacred. And in a culture that's increasingly isolated and transactional, even small acts of kindness stand out. Civility matters. Compassion matters. Simply showing up, paying attention, being present—these aren't extraordinary acts, but in a world that often feels cold and guarded, basic kindness shines like a bright light.

Even in our exhaustion, loneliness, and pain, something sacred happens when we turn our eyes outward. It doesn't erase what we're going through. But it reorients us. It loosens the grip of self-focus and reminds us: We're not the only ones in the wilderness.

Sometimes the very thing that begins to lift us is the decision to love someone else through their pain—while we're still carrying our own. Because wilderness living has a way of turning us inward. Struggle makes us retreat. We get consumed with our own survival, our own grief, our own fear. And that's understandable. But if we stay there too long, our world gets small.

But what if one of the most healing things you could do in your wilderness…is walk with someone in theirs? Not to ignore your pain. Not to fake strength. But because even in your deficit, God can move through you. You don't need to be healed to help. You don't need to have answers to offer presence.

Love doesn't have to be loud or certain or impressive. Sometimes it just looks like showing up when it would be easier to disappear. Sitting in silence. Sending the text. Asking the second question. Remembering the day. Being there when it matters.

Love is faithful. That's what makes it holy.

This isn't simply a concept. I've seen it up close—in my own story. Going from my wife's quiet heartbreak and sobs in the dark. Going from the silence of shame—not wanting to face what I'd done. To something that at the time didn't seem possible: restoration.

It wasn't immediate. It wasn't easy. But through forgiveness from her, vulnerability from me, counseling, and ongoing transparency—we found healing. Slowly. Through the power of grace and the practice of presence.

And we didn't do it alone. We had community. Friends who walked with us. Who helped me process my sin and shame. Who helped her grieve and rebuild. People who didn't flinch at our brokenness. People who stayed.

And maybe the most surprising grace of all: My wife, Stacy, has become my fiercest advocate. My primary protector in this struggle. She prays for me. Checks in with me. When I feel temptation rise, I can tell her. Not in fear, but in honesty. She listens. She stays.

That kind of restoration isn't flashy. It doesn't make headlines. But it's real. And it's holy.

Faithfulness doesn't always look impressive. More often, it's quiet. Unnoticed. Inconvenient. It shows up in the small, ordinary moments—the ones no one else sees but somehow make you feel less alone.

None of these things solve the struggle. But they remind us we're not invisible. We're not meant to carry life alone. These are the little ways we carry one another's burdens. Sometimes in the heavy seasons. Sometimes in the everyday exhaustion.

This is what it means to be the body of Christ—not alwaysheroic, but always devoted. We don't need more impressive people. We need more faithful ones. The kind who stay. The kind who notice. The kind who show up not just when the bottom drops out—but when the dishwasher floods or the kid throws up on the way to church or someone's just had a really discouraging Tuesday.

So find your place. Find your people. Align your life with what you value—not just what's easy. Spur one another on toward love and good deeds. Not through forced optimism or shallow smiles, but by becoming a safe place for one another's pain. A place where people can fall apart and still be met with warmth.

We need people who will walk with us in weakness. And we need to become those people for others. Because in this wilderness life, everything will tell you to isolate. To self-protect. To shut it all down. But the Kingdom calls us to something deeper. Something better.

Don't give up meeting together. Don't give up on people. Don't give up on love just because it didn't go the way you hoped last time. You don't have to do everything. You don't have to be everything. But you can be faithful.

And faithful love—flawed, awkward, honest, present—is how we walk each other home. That's how we become the family Jesus died to create. Together, in the wilderness.

8. Holding On to Wholeness

Living With Peace When the Story's Not Done

"Peace I leave with you; my peace I give you. I do not give to you as the world gives. Do not let your hearts be troubled and do not be afraid" (John 14:27).

Seasons Change

In 2019, I spent fifteen days in Israel. One of those days took us deep into the Judean wilderness—behind the Mount of Olives, away from Jerusalem. The land stretched out in dry, echoing silence. Everything was brown—soft, muted earth tones in every direction. Hills worn down by time. Dry grass waving in the breeze. It felt peaceful. Not dramatic—just stripped back. Simple. Like there was nothing left to distract you.

But there was something about it that felt familiar—not geographically, but emotionally. Like I'd walked through this kind of space before in my own soul. That quiet emptiness. Seasons of life where everything looks the same, day after day. Where nothing seems to be growing, and the color feels faded. Just…dry. Still. Bare. Those in-between stretches where you're not falling apart, but you're not thriving either. You're functioning, showing up, but it feels like all the fruit has withered, and you're waiting for something new to break through the surface again.

Most of the year, the Judean wilderness looks beige and brown, quiet and dry. But there's a brief moment when the beige blooms. For about two weeks in early spring, the whole landscape shifts. The desert doesn't disappear—it just wakes up.

Search "the Judean wilderness in spring," and you'll see pictures that almost don't look real. The same dry hills burst with color. Wildflowers—reds, purples, yellows—scatter across the rocky slopes. Thin green grass pushes through the cracks like it's been waiting all year. Even the almond trees bloom soft white and pale pink against the hillsides. For a little while, it feels like something new is breaking through. It doesn't last long. Just a couple of weeks. Then it fades back into that dry, quiet brown.

The land doesn't change. The season does.

Maybe peace—real peace—is like that, too. Not something that shows up when everything gets better…but something that grows right in the middle of the barrenness. Sometimes it's obvious, sometimes hidden. Sometimes brief, sometimes it lingers. It can feel dry in one season and beautifully alive in the next. Unbearable for a while, then quietly blooming again.

The question isn't whether the wilderness will change—it's whether we'll learn to notice the signs of life when it does. Whether we'll learn to receive peace even when we don't feel it. Whether we'll let God teach us how to find *shalom*—not just when the valley is green, but even when it's barren.

Those spring blooms in the wilderness don't last long. They come quickly, quietly—almost like a whisper. If you're not paying attention, you might miss them altogether. But when they do appear, they take your breath for a moment. Not because they fix everything, but because they remind you that something good can still grow here.

Peace can be like that, too. It doesn't always come with fanfare. It doesn't always stay. Sometimes it shows up in brief, unexpected ways—a conversation that softens you, a deep breath that steadies you, a moment when you realize God is closer than you thought. And then it's gone again. The silence returns. The routine sets back in. The wilderness doesn't disappear just because something beautiful bloomed.

That's the tension, isn't it? We want peace to be a destination—a place we can settle into once life calms down. But what if peace is more seasonal than static? Because even when spring breaks through, winter isn't gone forever. The wilderness remains.

And yet—every one of us longs for peace. That desire cuts across every culture, every worldview, every life stage. The language might change, but the ache is the same. The Hindu seeks peace through detachment. The Muslim through submission. The Buddhist through quieting the mind. The humanist through progress and knowledge. The secular mind through comfort, distraction, or achievement. All relentlessly pursuing but rarely finding. Even the Christian talks about peace more than most—but still quietly wonders why it feels so elusive.

We all want it. We all feel the need for it. But we don't all agree on where to find it—or what it even is.

Is it calm? Control? Escape? Clarity? Is it the absence of conflict or the presence of something deeper?

Maybe the more important question is: What is true peace, really? And if it's not tied to everything going right, if it doesn't rise and fall with our circumstances—then what kind of peace can hold in the wilderness? Where does it come from? And how do we hold onto it in a life that won't stop shifting underneath us?

The Pattern of Peace

In the modern world, peace often means relief—emotional calm, fewer problems, a clean mental state, or a sense of control. We define peace by what's absent: no stress, no tension, no drama. But maybe we need to reframe our definition of peace. Biblical *shalom* is rooted not in what's missing—but in what's present. It's something far more powerful. And far more durable.

In Jewish culture, one of the most common greetings is *"shalom shalom."* It's not just a polite way to say hello or goodbye—it's a blessing layered with meaning. Repeating the word adds weight. It's a way of saying: full peace. Complete wholeness. Not just peace over your circumstances, but peace deep in your bones. Peace that holds in the cracks. It's the opposite of fragmented living. *Shalom shalom* means: "May you be made whole—through and through."

Shalom isn't just the absence of conflict or stress. It's the presence of wholeness—completeness, restoration, harmony. Relationally, it's peace between you and God, others, and yourself. Spiritually, it's deep trust in God's nearness. Emotionally, it's being anchored amid hard feelings.

It's the kind of peace where nothing is missing and nothing is broken. And it's exactly the kind of peace we long for in this life—because the wilderness, by nature, feels broken. Life gets loud. Scattered. Unpredictable. We feel fractured—like our soul, our emotions, even our faith are living in different rooms, trying to hold a conversation but never quite syncing. *Shalom* is what holds it all together.

What's remarkable is that Scripture doesn't describe this kind of peace as just a future ideal; instead, it's a present reality. Not because the pain goes away. Not because things finally resolve. But because God shows up. Peace isn't found in the absence of pain—it's found in the presence of God. That's what makes Jesus' words in John 14:27 so powerful:

"Peace I leave with you; my peace I give you. I do not give to you as the world gives. Do not let your hearts be troubled and do not be afraid."

He spoke these words in the Upper Room, just hours before His arrest. The disciples were already rattled—confused by His words, disturbed by the growing tension around them. The religious leaders were furious. Rome was watching. And Jesus knew what was coming next. But even with all that hanging in the air, He talked about peace. And He didn't offer peace instead of pain. He offered peace within it.

"My peace I give you." It's a gift. Not a self-help mantra or generic comfort. It's His peace—rooted in unwavering trust in the Father, shaped by intimacy, forged through surrender. And He gives it to His disciples in advance of their worst moment.

This peace doesn't erase suffering. It prepares you to walk through it. That's the difference.

The world offers peace by controlling circumstances—fixing the problem, slowing life down, numbing the discomfort, getting answers fast. And when that doesn't work, the peace it offers evaporates.

But Jesus doesn't give peace like the world gives. His peace isn't about conditions; it's about presence. It doesn't depend on everything changing around you. It depends entirely on the One who walks with you.

That's why Paul could write about *"the peace of God, which transcends all understanding"* (Philippians 4:7) from his Roman prison cell. His situation was far from ideal; but God's presence offered peace in the middle of it all.

I remember sitting with a friend once over coffee. We were simply catching up on life, and he shared some difficult situations: estrangement from his brother, a wife struggling with significant health issues, challenges at work. It was a hard season.

In response, I simply asked him, "But how's your heart?"

He paused…looked at me and said, "It's good, I'm doing good." I think he was surprised that the words came from his mouth.,Even more surprising was that he meant it. God's presence and peace were with him during the storms.

It's remarkable when that happens—when God's peace holds steady even in present chaos.

For many of us, the things that steal peace aren't always what's happening right now. More often, it's what already happened. The past has a way of following us into the present—sometimes loud, sometimes quiet. We carry what was said, what we did, what we lost. Regrets. Shame. Grief. And sometimes, without even realizing it, those things quietly sabotage any sense of peace we're trying to build.

"Forget the former things; do not dwell on the past. See, I am doing a new thing! Now it springs up; do you not perceive it? I am making a way in the wilderness and streams in the wasteland" (Isaiah 43:18-19).

I mean…These words look great framed on a wall in your kitchen next to a cross collage (It's a Southern thing). But in real life? When your mind won't stop replaying what you wish you'd done differently? When you're stuck in patterns you swore you'd grow out of? When regret still lingers like fog? They feel less like a promise and more like wishful thinking.

I'm sure they felt this way to Israel. God's people weren't on a spiritual high when Isaiah delivered this message. They were a people in exile. Tired. Displaced. Haunted by their choices. Their suffering wasn't just circumstantial—it was laced with failure and consequence. Yet God didn't shame them. He invited them to forget what they had been clinging to. To stop replaying what was behind them. God was doing something new—and He still is. Even here. Even now.

Shalom isn't achieved by perfecting your past. It's received by trusting that God is forming something new—even in the wilderness you didn't choose.

So what does peace look like here? Not theoretically. Not eventually. But right here.

Sometimes it looks like calm. But more often, it looks like reckless trust. Sometimes it's the quiet strength to keep going. Sometimes it's the breath that reminds you you're not alone. Sometimes it's joy that somehow sits beside your grief without needing to be resolved.

That's why *shalom* is so radical. It's not a detour around the wilderness. It's a stream that cuts right through it. True peace isn't the absence of discomfort. It's the presence of God. Sometimes it's trust that holds steady while your heart still aches. Sometimes it's quiet strength when the answers haven't come. Sometimes it's joy that coexists with sorrow.

Isaiah puts it like this: *"The fruit of that righteousness will be peace; its effect will be quietness and confidence forever…in undisturbed places of rest"* (32:17-18).

That's what we're after—not a fleeting moment to capture, but a presence to walk with. Not peace that comes when the wilderness ends, but peace that takes root in the middle of it. That's the invitation of this chapter—to learn how to receive that kind of peace. Not by escaping the wilderness, but by staying rooted in it. And discovering that even here, even now, we can be whole.

Peace Be With You…

Of course, even after we name what peace is and where it comes from, that doesn't mean it's easy to live in. *Shalom* sounds beautiful in theory. But in practice, it gets tested in quiet and unseen ways. Especially in the wilderness. Especially when life doesn't let up. Some days, peace feels like something you brush up against briefly…and then lose again. Other days, it feels like a memory. Like something you once had but haven't felt in a long time.

That's because this wilderness life doesn't stay in one emotional gear. It moves. It shifts. One day you feel steady, the next you're overwhelmed by things you thought you had already worked through. Peace has to take on different forms in different seasons. There's an ebb and flow to it—a rhythm that's hard to notice until you name it.

Maybe that's where the idea of the changing seasons becomes helpful. The writer of Ecclesiastes said, *"There is a time for everything, and a season for every activity under the heavens…a time to plant and a time to uproot…a time to mourn and a time to dance… a time to tear and a time to mend"* (3:1-2, 4, 7). Peace isn't bound to one of those seasons. It shows up differently in each one.

There isn't a perfect metaphor for peace. But the concept of changing seasons gives us language for something we all feel. A way to name what's happening underneath the surface when we can't quite explain why peace feels distant or why hope feels fragile.

What if we could change our expectations and stop demanding that peace look the same all the time?

Winter in the Wilderness

Sometimes the wilderness feels like winter—quiet, still, empty. Everything looks bare. The world around you can feel cold and silent. God seems distant. Your prayers don't provide clarity or comfort, and you're not sure anything is growing at all.

Beneath the frozen ground, however, something is happening. Winter is not a wasted season. It's a time of rest, of dormancy, of hidden preparation. It strips life down to its essentials. The noise fades. The distractions thin out. And if we allow it, winter can be a time of restoration, of reorientation, even of healing that happens slowly, invisibly, deep beneath the surface.

But it takes work to stay warm. When the emotional and spiritual landscape feels barren, it's tempting to go cold, to feel numb, or assume God is gone. But what if we could see winter as preparation rather than punishment? *Shalom* in winter is often found in choosing to keep showing up—with your questions, your sadness, your empty prayers. It's curling closer to the fire of God's presence, even when you can't feel the heat yet.

We all know that feeling: when it's cold outside and we instinctively reach for comfort. A blanket. A warm drink. A familiar chair near the fire. Something in us longs to be surrounded, wrapped, protected. And that's where peace can show up, too.

Shalom in winter might look like sitting in silence—not expecting answers, but simply letting your soul breathe in the quiet. It may be reading through an old journal to see how God has met you in past seasons. It might be a Post-it note on your computer or dashboard with a scripture that reminds you of God's presence and power. It's daily reminding yourself he is working even when you can't see it. These small acts of trust become sacred in winter. They aren't escapes—they are anchors.

It's important to prepare ahead for winter. Developing spiritual rhythms. Building intentional community. These practices deepen your roots before the frost arrives. And in those times when winter does crash in suddenly, you're not left defenseless. You can still gather what you need and draw close.

You don't just survive winter by waiting for it to be over. You thrive by letting it slow you down. By letting it teach you how to rest without guilt. How to wait without rushing. How to trust that what looks like nothing is often the beginning of something sacred. Peace in winter may feel slow and deep. But it will settle in beside you if you make space for it. Sometimes *shalom* is simply the warmth of knowing you are not alone in the cold.

This is where we learn the discipline of stillness that Isaiah talked about: *"In repentance and rest is your salvation, in quietness and trust is your strength…"* (30:15). Like Israel, we often "would have none of it." We manage. We fix. We scramble for outcomes. And all the while, God is saying: "Stop. Return. Rest. Trust Me."

Stillness isn't passivity. It's not apathy. It's faith. It's choosing to stay when everything in you wants to run. It's listening when all you want to do is solve. It's receiving instead of controlling. Stillness anchors us—not because the wilderness becomes easy, but because we begin to see we're not alone in it.

Spring in the Wilderness

Spring in the wilderness doesn't show up with fanfare. It sneaks in. You don't always notice it right away. It's a moment of laughter after weeks of feeling blah. It's a random morning where you actually want to get out of bed. It's a walk outside where the air hits differently—like something's shifting, even if you can't explain what.

You're not out of the woods, but something in you starts to stir. And for the first time in a while, you wonder if maybe things aren't as stuck as they seemed.

It's a season of beginnings. And beginnings are beautiful…but often fragile. Hope returns, but winter still lingers. You want to believe something new is happening. You want to trust the thaw. But you've been here before—just long enough to know how easily new life can wither. You've seen false starts. You've been disappointed before. So part of you is ready to step forward…and part of you keeps looking over your shoulder.

That's the tension of spring—everything feels possible, but nothing feels guaranteed. And if you live in Texas, spring also means allergies. It's the three beautiful days we get each year, ruined by itchy eyes, sneezing fits, and clouds of floating cottonwood seeds (I hate that tree). Even beauty can come with irritation. That's how spring feels sometimes: undeniably hopeful, but annoyingly inconsistent.

Maybe we need to see spring as courage, not confidence. *Shalom* in spring is not confidence—it's courage. It's the kind of peace that says, "Try again," even while your hands are still sore. It might not feel deep yet. But it's enough to begin. Sometimes peace in spring looks like planting small things without proof they'll bloom. It's showing up to the gym after months of "cheat days." Reaching out to a friend you haven't talked to for too long. Opening your Bible not because you feel holy—but because you're hungry. It's not sexy. But it's real. There can be joy in spring—but also real fear. Peace doesn't mean you're no longer afraid of disappointment. It just means disappointment doesn't get the final say.

And when *shalom* starts to grow here, it can feel like wonder returning. You may find yourself watching the trees again. Letting music move you. Letting yourself laugh. Letting yourself believe that maybe, just maybe, something new is sprouting.

You can't rush spring. It grows one inch at a time. The peace of spring isn't a bold declaration—it's a nod "yes" to a God who is making things new—even when it's slow, even when you're uncertain, even when you can't yet see what's ahead.

This is what faith often looks like in spring—not bold or certain, but willing to try. Faith that doesn't wait to feel strong before it moves forward.

Summer in the Wilderness

Summer arrives with intensity. The days are long. The light is bright. There is fruit, yes—but there is also heat. Pressure. Fatigue. It's the season where everything is growing…and everything feels stretched. Some days are full of joy. You feel alive, connected, purposeful. Like the momentum you've been waiting for is finally here. Other days are just hot and heavy—thick with exhaustion. The growth is real, but it's costly. The work is relentless. Sometimes it feels like your soul is sweating.

It's the season of doing—of bearing fruit, of pushing through. But it's also the season where peace can feel lost beneath all your productivity. Where responsibilities can pile up. Where everything feels urgent. Where it's easy to confuse motion with depth. And summer can also mean sunburns—even when you've got SPF 50, a little shade, and your best plans and intentions. You still end up fried.

That's the tension: Good things are happening. Growth is visible. But if you're not careful, the pace starts to outrun your depth. The fruit multiplies, but your soul dries out. You start saying "yes" to everything—because it all seems important—until you're overextended and spiritually dehydrated.

But summer isn't just about productivity. It's also a season of play. Of fun. *Shalom* doesn't only show up in stillness—it can show up in celebration, too. Sometimes this peace looks like jumping in a pool, eating popsicles with your kids, going to a baseball game, planning a picnic, or laughing until your face hurts.

Lightness matters. Delight matters. Laughter isn't a detour from your spiritual life—it's often part of the healing.

So yes, *shalom* in summer might look like perseverance—like the stubborn determination to keep going when your tank is on empty. But it also can be choosing fun, intentionally. Stepping away from the grind. Prioritizing delight. Saying "no" without guilt. Creating space to play, even when everything feels important.

Peace is learning to rest before you break down. To let your fruitfulness flow from your rootedness—not your hustle. To trust that God is more interested in who you're becoming than what you're producing. Because *shalom* in summer doesn't mean stopping everything—it means staying grounded in the middle of everything. Letting your roots go deep enough that you can keep growing without falling apart. And when peace shows up, it might sound like this: Slow down. Drink some water. Take a walk. Laugh. You're allowed to rest—even while things are growing.

This is where we learn what Jesus modeled—stepping away from the crowds, even when the needs were endless. Even when people were disappointed. Even when it looked like he was wasting opportunities. Because He knew that ministry flows from intimacy, not duty. That fruitfulness comes from staying connected to the vine, not from trying harder.

Sometimes summer requires us to pull on the reigns when life is at full steam. To notice the warning signs—when we're running on fumes, when prayer feels like another task, when we're too tired to enjoy the fruit being produced. The discipline isn't just in the doing, but in the pausing. In stepping away before we break down, not after.

Fall in the Wilderness

Fall is the season of letting go. Of releasing what once was. The trees shed what they can no longer carry. Once-vibrant leaves lie in piles on the ground. The harvest winds down. It's not always clear if you're losing something…or being prepared for something new.

There's beauty here, for sure. Golden light. Crisp air. But there also can be a sense of loss underneath it. Fall carries the weight of transition. It's a season of reflection—of remembering and releasing. The wilderness in fall is honest. It doesn't pretend things are fine. It invites you to lay things down, to take inventory of what no longer fits, what has run its course, what needs to be buried before winter comes.

Fall is full of goodbyes. Some expected, some sudden. Some painful, some overdue. And *shalom* in this season might look like making peace with that. It's not about pretending the losses don't hurt—it's about letting yourself grieve them honestly, with God. It's recognizing that letting go doesn't mean failure—it means trusting that your story isn't finished, even if a chapter is.

This is the season for soul decluttering. For releasing expectations, timelines, titles, relationships, roles, habits, even dreams that once felt central. Not because they didn't matter—but because God is doing something new. And new growth often requires clearing space.

Shalom in fall might not feel light or easy. It might look like sitting with what you've lost instead of rushing to replace it. It might look like finally releasing what you've been holding too tightly. Sometimes peace looks like accepting the season you're in. Not fighting to get back what was. Not forcing what's next. Just being honest in the in-between.

And there's holiness in that. There's healing in release. Yet fall isn't just about what's falling away. It's also about what's being gathered. What's been growing beneath the surface. What's ready to be harvested—not for your striving, but for your sustenance. This season teaches us that peace isn't always about holding on. Sometimes it's found in letting go. And trusting that the ground knows what to do with the things we lay down.

The seasons change, but God doesn't. Through the stripped-back quiet of winter, the tentative stirring of spring, the overwhelming intensity of summer, and the letting-go of fall—He remains.

Putting Together the Pieces of Peace

Every season in the wilderness is a mixed bag—joy and fatigue, beauty and burden, hope and heartache. The seasons don't always follow predictable patterns: we find glimpses of light even in winter, and sometimes feel unexpected heaviness in the midst of summer. Most of the time, we carry all of it at once.

But here's the thread that holds through it all: God is there in every season. Not just watching from a distance. Not waiting for you to get through it. He's present. At work. In the silence, in the sunburns, in the letting go, in the fragile new beginning. And in each one, He keeps offering the same gift over and over again—peace.

Not peace as a concept. Peace as a person. Spoiler alert: *Jesus is the gift of peace. And the Spirit is the gift of presence.* We may not always feel Him. But He's there. Shaping. Holding. Speaking. The question isn't, "Is God here?" It's, "How do we learn to see Him in the season we're in?"

Because even in the wilderness—maybe especially in the wilderness—God is not hiding. He's revealing. But knowing that and feeling it are two different things. This is often where *shalom* begins to take root. Not in resolution, but right in the middle of the tension. Real *shalom* isn't handed out like a reward. It's forged. Grown. Formed slowly in the fire. It rises not when everything's fixed, but when we stop running. When we stop trying to hold everything together and start trusting that maybe we don't have to. When we see peace as a process rather than a prize.

That's where spiritual practices become essential—not as rigid formulas, but as flexible anchors that hold us steady regardless of the season. What prayer looks like in winter might be different than in summer, but the practice itself remains.

There's no formula, but there are ways we can posture ourselves to receive better. Just like tuning a radio or leaning in to catch a quiet voice across a noisy room, here are a few gentle rhythms that can help us become more attentive:

Immerse yourself in Scripture. If you want to know what God sounds like, start with what He's already said. The Bible isn't just an ancient text—it's a living voice. When everything else is unclear, His Word remains steady. You don't need to have a rigid plan. Pray one psalm all week. Read one chapter each day, or every other day. Listen to Scripture on an app while you're driving or walking. Let it settle. Let it speak. This is about relationship, not research or a to-do list.

Anchor yourself in His promises. Our feelings change. His character doesn't. When you feel distant or unsure, return to what you do know. Write down the promises of God. Read them out loud. Memorize what you can. Let them shape what silence can't explain. In the wilderness, promises become anchors—not because they change our circumstances, but because they remind us who holds them. When everything feels unstable, His Word remains unshakable.

Curate sacred spaces. God's whisper is easy to miss when our minds are cluttered. Make room for quiet—leaving your phone in another room, sitting with a verse for five minutes, going on a walk without headphones. Stillness doesn't come naturally, especially in a culture that rewards constant motion. But it creates space for presence. You're not trying to manufacture a spiritual experience—you're simply making room for God to meet you where you are. Sometimes the most profound encounters happen in the most ordinary moments of quiet.

Pay attention to how God speaks through others. He often uses people—trusted friends, spiritual mentors, even unexpected conversations—to echo His heart. A good rule of thumb for me: The person I probably don't want to talk to is often the very person I need to talk to. He also works through circumstances, timing, opportunities, and closed doors. Nothing is accidental in the Kingdom.

Learn how you naturally connect with God. We don't all hear Him the same way. For me, it's music—my life has a constant soundtrack, and God often speaks through lyrics that meet me where I am. For my wife, it's nature. For others, it's deep study or conversation around a table with good food and good wine. Where does His voice tend to resonate with you? That's something to notice and lean into.

As you practice these things, try not to fixate on what God *isn't* saying. Pay attention to what He has said. What He is doing. What has remained steady—even when everything else feels shaky. And above all: Keep listening. Keep seeking. You don't need to chase clarity. Just stay near.

I tend to be a little thick-headed and stubborn. Maybe that's why God has had to lead me back to this truth more times than I'd like to admit. Again and again, He strips away my false peace—the illusions of control, the things I cling to for security—and gently redirects my gaze back to Him. Not because He's disappointed, but because He knows where real peace lives.

Israel was thick-headed and stubborn, too. That's why God kept saying the same things in different ways. It's why, at their lowest point—exiled, worn out, buried in consequence and silence—He didn't scold them or give up. He spoke. Not after they recovered. Right in the middle of it all. He told them He was already moving. Already making a way in the wilderness. Already carving out streams in the wasteland.

That's what makes it so profound: Long before you see the water, God is already digging the streambed. Maybe that's where hope really starts. Not when the landscape changes, but when you begin to believe something is happening beneath the surface. Something you can't see yet. Something God is shaping even here. Even now.

There's a pattern that shows up again and again in Scripture: Peace isn't something we manufacture—it's something that grows. Isaiah described it like this: *"The fruit of that righteousness will be peace; its effect will be quietness and confidence forever"* (32:17).

Fruit means process. Time. Often underground, often unseen. Grown through seasons that feel slow, dry, or unresolved. And sometimes we miss peace because we're trying to force it. To fix everything around us. To chase clarity, relief, or control. But *shalom* doesn't come through control. It comes through trust. It's the quiet result of staying rooted in the One who holds you—especially when nothing else makes sense.

So what do we do when peace feels elusive?

When God seems quiet?

When the wilderness life doesn't let up?

It's not about striving harder. We start by looking again. Not for a dramatic rescue, but for His presence in the ordinary.

Peace That Passes Understanding

We started this chapter asking what true peace could look like in an unfinished story. We've learned that maybe we need to change how we see everything—our understanding of peace, our expectations of how it arrives, our timeline for when it should show up. Peace isn't seasonal relief. It's a constant Presence.

Whether you're in the stripped-back quiet of winter, the tentative stirring of spring, the overwhelming productivity of summer, or the letting-go of fall, the invitation remains the same. It's the same invitation Jesus gave His disciples that night in the Upper Room: *"Peace I leave with you; my peace I give you. I do not give to you as the world gives"* (John 14:27).

That offer hasn't changed. The peace Jesus gives doesn't wait for our lives to calm down. It shows up in the middle of the swirl. It doesn't depend on outcomes or relief. It's not a finish line we finally cross—it's the quiet companion we walk with. The reminder that we're not alone.

Some of the deepest peace didn't show up when everything got better. It came in moments when nothing had changed externally—but something had shifted inside. Your friend who lost his job still wakes up early to sit with God in the quiet. No answers, no breakthrough—just showing up. And somehow, his spirit stays steady.

That woman walking through chronic illness still manages to ask others how they're doing. She's not in denial—she just carries a kind of calm that doesn't match her circumstances, and it makes you lean in and wonder where it comes from. The neighbors who buried their child find themselves laughing around the dinner table one night—not because the pain is gone, but because joy has quietly pulled up a chair beside the grief.

This is the kind of peace Jesus offers. Not all at once. Not loudly. But deeply. Quietly. Sustainably.

Peace is learning to stop chasing change and start receiving presence—not because the problem disappears, but because God is in the room with you while it lingers. *Shalom* isn't built on outcomes—it's built on intimacy. Peace isn't the prize at the end of your wilderness; it's the presence of God with you in the middle of it.

So what does it look like to live from that kind of peace? Slowing down enough to notice Him again. Praying honestly—not performing, just showing up. Sabbath—not because the work is done, but because your soul needs to breathe. Community—being known by people who can carry the silence with you.

And above all, it looks like rest—not just in your pace, but in your identity. Jesus said, *"Come to me, all you who are weary and burdened, and I will give you rest… You will find rest for your souls"* (Matthew 11:28–29).

Rest isn't just a pause. It's a Person. Peace isn't something you achieve—

it's someone you trust. You don't have to wait for the season to end to find peace. You don't need to have every answer, or feel strong, or fix what's broken. You just have to come. Because even here—even now—*shalom* is still possible.

IV. Wonder of the Wilderness

"Ring the bells that still can ring. Forget your perfect offering. There is a crack in everything. That's how the light gets in."
— *Leonard Cohen "Anthem" (1992)*

9. The Shimmer in the Shadows

Embracing Beauty in the Wilderness

"But we have this treasure in jars of clay to show that this all-surpassing power is from God and not from us... Therefore we do not lose heart. Though outwardly we are wasting away, yet inwardly we are being renewed day by day"
(2 Corinthians 4:7, 16).

The Treasure and the Tension

No one dreams of burying the person they love most. And yet this is the wilderness terrain we must navigate. Life in a broken world doesn't play by our rules. But even in the darkest places, God still writes stories—not to tie things up with a bow, but to reveal beauty in the driest soil.

Chris and Julie met on a blind date. A friend who knew them both decided to play matchmaker. It worked. There was something simple and strong between them from the start. They got married in 1998, had four children, and built a life anchored in Jesus and their family. Life wasn't flashy—but it was full.

Heading into the final stretch of parenting, just a few years from an empty nest, they planned for their next season—travel, ministry, grandkids. The kind of dreams that take decades to build. But then something shifted.

Julie began feeling unusually tired—foggy, unsteady in ways that didn't add up. At first, it was easy to write off. A rough week. Stress. Nothing serious. But those moments kept piling up. Something wasn't right. So they went in for tests—just to be safe. One test led to another, and another until everything changed. A tumor. Glioblastoma. Brain cancer. It was the same kind of tumor that had just taken a friend of theirs. They knew the odds. They knew the brutality. But they also knew God. And so they fought—with prayers, with treatment, with hope.

Julie underwent major brain surgery—full of risk and fragile faith. It became a cycle—brief moments of hope followed by deeper discouragement. Still, they held on—to Jesus and to each other. To the possibility of a miracle. "Lord, I know You can do this," Chris would pray. And they meant it. Every time. They believed. But healing didn't come the way they hoped. In February 2017, Julie went to be with Jesus.

Chris found himself staring at a future he never imagined—widowed, with four grieving children, and a life that felt completely dismantled. Everything familiar had been upended. The plans they'd made, the rhythms they'd lived, the comfort of partnership—it was gone. And yet, God was present. Not in sweeping gestures or grand displays, but in steady, quiet provision. He showed up in unexpected ways—through family, through friends, through a church that refused to let them walk alone. They were held together by small mercies, ordinary faithfulness, and a grace that showed up day by day. It wasn't fast. It wasn't flashy. But it was enough.

Among those in the church who offered support during Julie's battle were Jason and Linsie. Over the years, they had crossed paths with Chris and Julie often—sharing life in the same church community. Linsie had always admired Julie: her love for Jesus, the way she served her family, her steady faith, the quiet strength she carried through the diagnosis. Even as the future unraveled, Julie's trust in God never seemed to waver. It left a mark that Linsie wouldn't forget.

Linsie and Jason met in college and married in 2006. From the beginning, their life together felt full of momentum and purpose. They had two young children and were deeply rooted in their church—serving, leading, and investing in the lives of others. Jason had a magnetic way with people. He noticed those on the margins. He made people feel seen. He was a builder—not just of ideas, but of community. Their home was full of laughter, late-night talks, open doors, and shared dreams. It wasn't perfect, but it was deeply good. They felt like true partners, running after the same vision together.

Then Jason started to feel pain in his hip. What seemed minor became persistent. Tests revealed a rare form of incurable cancer. Jason was forty-one. Vibrant. Healthy. Thriving in his career. There was no way to make sense of it. But they did what they knew to do. They fought—through treatment, through prayer, with all the faith they could muster. It was a blur of doctors, scans, chemo, exhaustion, and waiting.

Because it was the height of COVID, Linsie walked much of that road alone. She sat through appointments without Jason. She received life-altering news in rooms where no one else could be with her. The weight was unbearable. Through it all, they kept asking God for a miracle. They knew He could heal. They believed it with everything they had. But healing didn't come. Jason went to be with Jesus just eight months after the initial diagnosis.

Linsie was left with a house full of memories and two children whose worlds had been turned upside down. She didn't know what came next. Grief doesn't hand out instructions. But God brought people—family, friends, a church that walked with her through the chaos.

One of those people was Marsha, a widow from their community who showed up with quiet understanding and consistent presence. She didn't try to fix anything—but she understood. She sat with Linsie, walked alongside her, and became a steady presence in a season that had no roadmap. Slowly, life began to take shape again—not neatly, not without setbacks, but with steps that started to resemble movement. It would never be a return to what was—but it could be the beginning of something new, rooted in love, shaped by loss, and open to whatever God might grow next.

Learning to Lament

The wilderness invites us to something unexpected. Not surrender. Not escape. Not denial. But presence. It asks us to stay awake to both the pain and the wonder. To hold sorrow and shimmer in the same hand. To look struggle straight in the eye without pretending it's not there—and still be open to the possibility that beauty is, too.

And one of the ways we practice this gaze—this refusal to let the pain define the story—is through lament. Not as a detour from faith, but as its most faithful expression. It becomes a lens—a way of holding space for what hurts while still noticing what's holy.

Lament isn't wallowing. It's refusing to go silent. It's grief that still speaks to God. The Psalms are full of it—honest cries, raw questions, emotional unedited-ness: *How long, O Lord? Why have You forsaken me? My God, are You listening?*

These aren't sanitized prayers. They're survival prayers. And still—they turn toward God, not away, with their their eyes lifted up.

That's the power of lament: It keeps the relationship intact, even when everything else is falling apart. The prophet in Lamentations said it plainly: *"I remember my affliction and my wandering, the bitterness and the gall…my soul is downcast within me"* (3:19-20).

He's not minimizing what hurts—he's naming it. But right in the middle of that honesty, he added: *"Yet this I call to mind and therefore I have hope. Because of the Lord's great love we are not consumed, for His compassions never fail"* (v. 21-22).

He holds grief and hope in the same breath. And that's what we are invited to do, too. Hope doesn't cancel sorrow. It sits beside it. This is the heart of seeing beauty in the wilderness—not avoiding grief, but noticing God within it.

The wilderness doesn't care about your title, your income, your Instagram presence, or your theology degree. It comes for all of us. And sometimes it stays longer than we ever imagined it could. But we've been taught—especially in faith spaces—to reach for spiritual language as a kind of emotional shortcut, trying to move past the ache instead of walking through it. That's called "spiritual bypassing"—using spiritual practices and beliefs to avoid dealing with unresolved emotional wounds, relational issues, and personal pain. Instead of facing grief, anger, or fear directly, people "float above" their suffering in the name of faith or inner peace. It looks holy—but it's actually avoidance.

We slap Romans 8:28 on someone's tragedy like a Band-Aid. We say things like, "God's got a plan" or, "Everything happens for a reason" when someone's heart is breaking in front of us. We over-spiritualize and under-feel. We quote scripture like armor to deflect our actual feelings. We numb ourselves with Christian clichés instead of letting God meet us in the feelings and frustrations. Scripture is meant to sustain us, not shield us from reality. God's Word should anchor us in truth while we wrestle honestly with what hurts.

Lament isn't about pretending it's all okay. It's not asking us to put on a brave face and call the pain a blessing. It's inviting us to look deeper—to trust that even in sorrow, even in hardship, there is something being formed in us that couldn't be formed any other way. This is the difference between bypassing and lamenting. Bypassing skips the pain to get to the promise. Lament goes through the pain with honesty, with trembling, with trust.

You don't have to pretend you're not wrestling. God already knows. From the very beginning, His question has always been, "Where are you?" Not to shame us, but to draw us out. To call us into presence. To remind us that even in the wilderness—especially in the wilderness—we were never meant to walk alone. And He meets us *in* the wrestling. Not just after it.

So name what hurts. Acknowledge the lies. Let the struggle surface. You're not less spiritual for asking hard questions. You're not less faithful for feeling disoriented. Sometimes being honest is the most faithful thing you can do. And it's here—in this raw, unfiltered space—that we begin to discover what kind of God comes to meet us.

The enemy whispers that your questions disqualify you, that no one would understand. So we stay silent. But the longer we're isolated, the deeper the lies begin to settle. They become internal. Familiar. Eventually, they start to sound like us.

But God never asked us to fake it. He asked us to trust Him. And trust always requires honesty. With Him, with ourselves, and yes…with others we can trust.

Jesus in Gethsemane

There is a moment in His story that lives right inside this same tension—Gethsemane. The garden where grief and glory collided. We tend to think of the cross as the place of ultimate sacrifice—and it is. But Gethsemane was the place of surrender. The place of wrestling. The place where love chose to stay, even in the ache.

Alone in the shadows of olive trees, Jesus fell to His knees, overcome with sorrow. Matthew said His *"soul was overwhelmed with sorrow to the point of death"* (26:38). He wasn't shrinking back from the cross physically—He was holding the weight of cosmic isolation, injustice, and coming separation from the Father. With trembling words He prayed, *"Father, if there is any other way…"* And His sweat fell like drops of blood.

This was not weakness. It was love refusing to pretend. He didn't bypass the pain. He named it. He felt it. He carried it in His body. And even then—even there—He surrendered: *"Yet not as I will, but as you will"* (v. 39).

Not because the struggle was gone. Not because the questions were resolved. But because His love was deeper than the pain.

Then as He hung on the cross—broken, bleeding, mocked—beauty still emerged. In one of His final breaths, Jesus looked down and gave His mother and His friend to one another: *"Woman, behold, your son!…Behold, your mother"* (John 19:26-27, ESV). Even there, while the world unraveled, something beautiful was being knit together. Connection. Care. Love—in the middle of the breaking.

The mystery we're invited to hold is that grief and grace, sorrow and beauty, can occupy the same space. Gethsemane and Golgotha both teach us this: Pain is real—but beauty can rise right in the middle of the ashes. And surrender does not mean defeat. Sometimes it's the doorway to the deepest kind of life.

Beautifully Normal

Paul wrote, *"But we have this treasure in jars of clay, to show that this all-surpassing power is from God and not from us"* (2 Corinthians 4:7). Glory and fragility, beauty and ordinary, side by side. Something holy, something eternal, something powerful entrusted to something that can crack.

And that is exactly what this wilderness life feels like. Fragile. Brittle. Worn.

It's how most of us feel after walking through suffering for any length of time. But our busted and broken vessels hold infinite treasure—the presence of God Himself. God doesn't wait for us to be whole to inhabit us. He chooses to dwell in the cracks, in the worn places, in the very fragility we spend so much energy trying to hide or escape.

There are days when we don't even feel like jars—just pieces. Shards. Barely holding together. Paul didn't apologize for the fragility or offer tips to become a stronger vessel. Instead, he owned it. And insisted—it's part of the design.

It's not despite our weakness that God moves—it's through it. In fact, it's intentional. The very fact that glory is housed in something fragile shows that the power is from God and not from us. If the vessel were impressive, we might be tempted to credit the vessel. But when the cracks are obvious—when the container itself looks like it can't hold the weight—then the treasure shines more clearly.

Our weakness and brokenness don't obscure God's power. It highlights it. That truth alone should reframe much of what we fear in suffering. We assume weakness disqualifies us. That being cracked means being useless. But what if we learned that fragility is the very place where treasure becomes visible? What if it's not the polished, self-sufficient, got-it-all-together life that reveals God's power—but the fragile, dependent, barely-making-it kind?

We don't just lay down and give up, however. Though we are weak, we are never abandoned. He articulates it in a series of paradoxes: *"We are hard pressed on every side, but not crushed; perplexed, but not in despair; persecuted, but not abandoned; struck down, but not destroyed"* (2 Corinthians 4:8-9).

You can hear the lived experience in those words. This isn't theoretical. It's the voice of someone who knew what it was to be pressed to the breaking point—but never broken beyond repair.

The point isn't that we won't face pressure, confusion, or pain. The point is that in all of it, we are held. Though we are fragile, we are never crushed. Though we are confused, we are never without hope. Though we feel alone, we are never truly abandoned. Though we are wounded, we are never destroyed.

If you've spent any time in wilderness seasons, you know this space. The days when the questions outnumber the answers. The nights when grief wakes you before dawn. The moments when your chest carries a weight words can't explain. And yet Paul refuses to let those realities be the whole story. Yes, the pain is real. But it's not the end of the story—it's where the deeper story begins: *"Though outwardly we are wasting away, yet inwardly we are being renewed day by day"* (v. 16).

This is the paradox at the heart of wilderness living. Everything visible—our bodies, our circumstances, our carefully laid plans—may be unraveling. The dreams we built, the relationships we treasured, the version of ourselves we thought we'd become by now—all of it can feel like it's falling apart.

But something else is happening beneath the surface. God is not fixing what's breaking on the outside, but forming something eternal on the inside. We are being prepared for something we can't yet see, shaped for a purpose that transcends our present pain. A renewal that doesn't come through grand moments or easy answers but through small, faithful mercies. Manna-sized portions. Just enough for today. The kind of formation that can only happen in the furnace of honest struggle.

Seeing the wilderness differently means seeing this tension differently—not as contradiction, but as mystery. We can hold both truths: We are wasting away *and* being renewed. We are fragile *and* filled with treasure. We are cracked *and* still capable of carrying glory.

And maybe this is one of the great miracles in the wilderness—that God's presence so often comes not in sweeping displays, but in quiet strength. Enough to breathe. To take one more step. To stay in the story. *"For our light and momentary troubles are achieving for us an eternal glory that far outweighs them all"* (v. 17).

It's the kind of sentence that doesn't come easily. You can almost imagine Paul pausing, his hand shaking a little as he wrote it. Maybe the Spirit had to whisper it first—and Paul had to trust it was true. Because he wasn't sheltered from sorrow. His life was marked by beatings, shipwrecks, betrayal, and loss. He knew what it meant to suffer. He knew what it cost to stay.

"Light and momentary." Really? Those aren't the words we would've chosen. They don't match the weight of what Paul endured. And they certainly don't match the grief many of us carry.

Chris and Linsie wouldn't call their suffering "light" or "momentary." They buried spouses. They parented through grief. They prayed prayers that seemed to return unanswered. And for us…the losses, the diagnoses, the unraveling of life as we thought it would be don't feel light. They feel crushing. Endless.

But Paul isn't minimizing the pain. He's not comparing pain to other pain, but pain to glory. To something deeper and longer and heavier than we can now imagine. Something eternal.

He's reminding us that suffering is not the end of the story. That pain may echo loudly, but it won't echo forever. And somehow—mysteriously, miraculously—our deepest sorrows are producing something greater than we can yet hold. Something that will last. Something that will matter forever.

It doesn't make it easier. It doesn't make it fair. But it makes it less meaningless. It invites us to trust that even when we can't trace the purpose, we are being formed into something sacred. Maybe that's the shift: seeing the wilderness not as punishment, but as formation.

If I'm honest, it feels like punishment, like failure, like almost anything other than what it is. My heart clamors for control, my mind races for solutions, my soul screams for this to just be over already. I want to fix it, escape it, explain it away, or at least understand why it has to hurt so much. But Paul says, "Deep breath. Look up."

"So we fix our eyes not on what is seen, but on what is unseen, since what is seen is temporary, but what is unseen is eternal" (v. 18).

This isn't just spiritual advice—it's intensely practical. And learning to see beauty in this wilderness—especially when everything visible is breaking—requires us to understand how vision actually works.

Target Fixation

I love dirt bikes. Always have. As soon as I could afford one—in my late twenties—I bought one. Correction: I bought one for me, one for my wife, and one for our then three-year-old son (with training wheels). Naturally, that also meant buying a toy hauler camper to haul the bikes…and, of course, a new truck to pull the camper. (Go big or go home, right?)

We started going camping about once a month with a group of eight to ten families. We'd set up camp in the high desert of California—wide open spaces, mountain trails, no cell service. Some of my favorite memories were made on those weekends—laughing around the campfire, riding for hours through rugged trails, watching the kids tear around camp on their little bikes. It was the perfect blend of adventure and rest.

One particular trip, we pulled in on a Thursday afternoon—got there about an hour before sunset. I was itching to ride. I could barely wait to unload the bikes. So, while everyone else was setting up camp, I decided to take a quick lap around a small loop trail that circled our campsite. It wasn't much—a few natural jumps, some small hills—but it would scratch the itch for the night. I tore out of camp way too fast, clicking through gears, racing toward the first jump. As soon as I left the ground, I realized—too late—that I had overshot it. I was going to land way off the intended line.

As I came down, my eyes locked onto a large yucca tree just to my right—something I absolutely needed to avoid. But I couldn't stop looking at it. And the more I stared at that tree, the more my bike seemed magnetically drawn to it. I tried to correct, but it was too late. I rode straight into it—crashing, dislocating my shoulder, and earning a nice little field trip to the ER thirty minutes down the road.

What I experienced is something well-known in motorcycle circles: *target fixation*. It's the phenomenon where your bike tends to go wherever your eyes are fixed. If you stare at the obstacle you're trying to avoid, you'll likely hit it. The only way to steer out of danger is to consciously look where you want to go. Your gaze determines your trajectory. And when fear locks your eyes onto the wrong thing, it's incredibly difficult to break free.

That's not just a riding principle. It's a life principle.

Keep Your Head Up

Paul's advice to *"fix our eyes not on what is seen, but on what is unseen"* (2 Corinthians 4:18) describes more than a spiritual idea—it points to a practice. Because learning to see beauty in this world—especially in the wilderness—is anything but passive. It's deliberate. Repetitive. Exhausting. Everything around us is designed to pull our gaze down.

Life's weight constantly drags our eyes toward the urgent, the loud, the painful. It happens in the daily stress, the late-night anxiety, the quiet disappointments that stack up like stones on our chest.

But it also happens in the culture we live inside. We are formed in a system where division is profitable. Where fear sells. Where outrage is a business model. Where algorithms are engineered to keep us reactive, distracted, angry, and exhausted.

Social media doesn't just reflect this reality—it amplifies it. Every time we scroll, we're swimming in a digital current designed to reinforce what's broken, what's threatening, what's ugly. And over time, it conditions our gaze. We start to live in spiritual target fixation—locked onto what wounds us, what divides us, what drains us. We lose sight of what's good, what's holy, what's eternal.

That's why fixing our eyes is sacred resistance. It is not an escape. It is not denial. It is the practice of presence.

The decision—time and again—to scan the horizon for shimmer, for goodness, for the face of God in the middle of the angst is like riding that dirt bike: If you stare at the fear, you'll steer straight into it. But if you learn to shift your gaze—even in the tension—you start to find a new trajectory. One that leads you toward life. Toward hope. Toward beauty that's still unfolding in the wilderness.

That's what it means to "fix your eyes." Not a one-time act of faith—but a daily discipline. A practiced gaze. A rhythm of continually turning toward what is unseen. Because in a world that constantly tries to pull us down, learning to lift our eyes is an act of courage. And an act of grace.

Fixing your eyes on the unseen doesn't look heroic. Most of the time, it looks ordinary. It might be opening your Bible and reading words that feel more like ink than revelation—but reading them anyway. It could be whispering a simple prayer on your drive to work. Lifting your hands in worship when your heart feels numb. Sometimes it's just choosing not to spiral when you're tired. Pausing—just for a breath—before reacting to the chaos of the day. Even that is an act of lifting your gaze.

It's not about pretending everything is fine. It's about choosing, moment by moment, to resist the gravity that pulls your eyes down. Because life will pull them down. The weight of the wilderness wants to lower your gaze, to tether you to what is urgent, painful, incomplete. But fixing your eyes is a prayer—sometimes barely uttered: *"Help me see You here."*

It's a rhythm. A quiet practice of remembering that beauty still lives here—even in this. Not to bypass pain or cover it in platitudes. But to anchor yourself in real hope. The decision to keep looking. Even when it would be easier to look away. The willingness to lift your eyes toward something deeper, truer, more eternal than whatever is pressing in.

And when you do—slowly, almost without realizing it—you begin to see differently. The cracks don't vanish, but they start to shimmer. The ache doesn't dissolve, but it makes space for something sacred. The wilderness doesn't become easy—but it becomes beautiful in ways you never expected.

Broken Beauty

Chris and Linsie's stories began to weave together long before either of them realized it. After Jason passed, Chris would occasionally reach out—popcorn on Thanksgiving, Christmas gifts for the kids. He knew the road Linsie was walking and simply wanted to be a friend along the way. But over time, a shift happened. When Chris would reach out—a holiday text, a quick check-in—something deeper began stirring beneath the surface. It wasn't planned. It wasn't dramatic. It just started to feel different. Eventually, it reached a point where he couldn't keep texting without being honest. So they met for coffee. He wasn't trying to persuade her of anything. He simply needed to express what was growing inside him. To speak it out loud. To let her decide what it meant.

Linsie wasn't ready—not yet. But she wasn't closed, either. She received his honesty with grace. They agreed to keep walking forward—not as a couple, but as friends navigating grief with open hands and mutual respect.

Over the next few months, something began to shift. Slowly, their relationship deepened. Trust formed. Affection grew. They continued walking carefully, deliberately—carrying a sacred awareness of all they had lost…and all that might still be possible.

Chris and Linsie got married in April 2022. Their wedding was rooted in remembrance, filled with tenderness, and marked by the kind of love that makes space for the past while stepping into the future. Pictures of Jason and Julie were everywhere. Their names were spoken; their absence, acknowledged; their impact, celebrated.

Their journey shows us what it means to reframe beauty in the wilderness—not as the absence of sorrow, but as something that can emerge right alongside it. Stories that don't tie things up with a bow. Grief that doesn't get erased. But somehow, in the ash and the loss, something beautiful grows—not in spite of the wilderness, but because of it.

The call of the wilderness is not to pretend the cracks aren't there, but to learn that cracked lives can still carry priceless treasure. Sometimes the most sacred beauty doesn't rise in power but in weakness. In the fragile places. In jars of clay.

In a Japanese art form called *kintsugi*, a broken piece of pottery isn't discarded or patched up to hide the damage. It's mended with gold. The cracks become part of the design—highlighted, honored, transformed into something even more beautiful than before. The bowl isn't restored to what it was; it becomes something new. Something resilient. Something redeemed.

That's what God does. He doesn't erase the breaks. He fills them. And somehow, our most wounded areas can become the very places His glory shines through. The treasure isn't diminished by our brokenness; it's revealed through it.

That doesn't mean we stop grieving. Or that the pain goes away. It means we begin to see it differently. We begin to see Him in it. We begin to see beauty where we never expected it to grow.

I've had a scar on my arm since I was a baby. Most people don't notice it anymore, but I still do. It's from an accident—scalding water that spilled when my mom tripped while holding me. Nothing dramatic. Nothing cinematic. Just a small, painful moment that left a permanent mark. I used to wish it had a better story. Something tougher. Something more heroic. Over the years, I may have told a few versions that made it sound a little cooler than it really was. But the truth is—like most scars—it came from something I didn't ask for. Something painful. Something that healed but never fully disappeared.

And that's the thing about scars. They don't go away.

We all carry scars. Some you can see; most you can't. But all of them—every mark, every memory, every stretch of skin where healing took place—speak of something we've lived through. And when we hide them, we hide the evidence that we survived. That God showed up. That beauty was possible after the breaking. That we're still here.

Our scars are not proof of failure; they're proof of faithfulness. They say: This broke me…but not completely. This wounded me…but not forever. This changed me…and yet, here I am. Learning to reframe our scars means seeing them not as weaknesses to be ashamed of, but as places where God's gold has filled the cracks.

And when we stop hiding the scars—when we let them tell their story—we discover that flourishing doesn't mean what we thought it did.

We tend to believe that flourishing means overcoming—pushing past pain and getting back to strength. But what if flourishing looks different? What if it's not triumph, but trust? Not resolution, but endurance? Flourishing can look like simply continuing to show up—with a limp. It can be praying when you're not sure anyone's listening. It's the quiet choice to stay rooted when everything in you wants to run.

This is the kind of hope wilderness life seeks—not a loud, polished, breakthrough kind of hope, but something quieter. Something more realistic. A hope that doesn't deny sorrow but makes space for beauty beside it.

This kind of hope doesn't arrive all at once. It's sustained through slow, rooted practices. Not silver bullets. Not quick fixes. But rhythms that keep you grounded when everything else feels shaky.

Chris and Linsie have learned to live this out. Now, as a blended family, they live with both joy and loss side by side. Their kids are learning to navigate the complexity. There's laughter. There's healing. There are still hard days. But there is also beauty—real beauty—not in spite of the suffering, but through it.

Chris and Linsie continue to serve others walking through grief. They speak honestly about what it means to live with loss. They don't pretend it's tidy. But they also don't accept that it's hopeless. They've learned to hold space for both sorrow and goodness in the same breath.

That tension eventually led Linsie and Marsha to launch Marsha's Heart—a ministry for women navigating the wilderness of grief. Just as God used Marsha's journey to walk Linsie through her own, now the three of them walk with others on a similar road. They show up not with answers, but with presence. With the kind of comfort that only comes from having lived it. Their scars have become their ministry. Their brokenness, their gift.

That's what it means to reframe beauty in the wilderness—to let our cracks become the very places where light gets in and love flows out. Not escaping the wilderness, not waiting for life to get easier, but learning to see beauty right here. To stay present. To stay open. To stay faithful, even when nothing around you feels resolved.

And maybe that's the quiet miracle of it all. Not that the cracks disappear, but that they can hold glory. Not that the ache dissolves, but that it can make space for something sacred. Like *kintsugi*—where the mended gold isn't hidden but honored. Where the broken places aren't weaknesses to be ashamed of, but the very places where beauty shines through.

That's how God meets us in this wilderness life. Not waiting for us to be whole—but filling the fractures with His grace. Not asking us to cover the scars—but using them to tell a story of mercy.

You may still feel fragile. That's okay. Fragile things can be faithful. And faithful things—when held in His hands—can be beautiful.

God doesn't discard what is fragile. He inhabits it. He is the gold that fills the cracks in us. He doesn't throw away the broken; He honors us. He doesn't despise the scars; He uses them. He doesn't wait until we're whole to love us; He meets us in the breaking.

Beautiful things can flourish—even in the wilderness. Especially when we learn to see through His eyes.

10. An Oasis in the Wilderness

How Our Leaks Let Living Water Flow

"Jesus answered, 'Everyone who drinks this water will be thirsty again, but whoever drinks the water I give them will never thirst. Indeed, the water I give them will become in them a spring of water welling up to eternal life'"
(John 4:13–14)

Anyone but Her

She's been through three marriages. The first one was the hardest—because the failure was hers.

She cheated.

It was impulsive and secret and slow-burning with guilt. At the time, she told herself she was lonely. Neglected. But deep down, she knew it wasn't just his absence that led her there—it was something broken in her. Something afraid of being unseen.

He left, and she didn't blame him. But from that point on, every relationship felt shadowed. Even when she tried to do better, she was still navigating life through the lens of her regret. She became emotionally guarded, terrified of being vulnerable, convinced that one mistake had rewritten her worth.

Her second marriage? She overcorrected. Became silent and passive, convinced she didn't have the right to complain. The relationship withered within the silence. The third was built on convenience and chemistry—two people with pasts trying to convince each other they were okay. It ended in shouting and shattered expectations.

Now, she's living with someone—not because she thinks it's good or right, but because she can't afford to be alone. She's not pretending anymore. She's just surviving. And she's doing it quietly.

It's a small town—and people talk. She hears the murmurs, the half-finished sentences. The glances, head tilts, awkward pauses that resume when she's out of earshot.

"Good thing you can order groceries online now," she jokes to herself. She hasn't shopped in person in a long time. Too many familiar faces. Too much potential of running into her past. Too much shame. She avoids the local coffee shop. She takes back roads to work. Anything to steer clear of people who've known her since she was a teenager—back when everything still felt whole and full of promise.

But nowhere is it more obvious than at church. They say hi. They smile. But when she walks past, she can feel it—their eyes on her back, the subtle shift in conversation, the sideways glances. She doesn't need to hear the words to know what's being said.

"I know I messed up. I've tried to repent. I've tried to start over. But grace feels like it belongs to people with cleaner stories."

"Sometimes I wonder if I'm too far gone."

For months, she lingered in her doubts. Going through the motions—work, bills, grocery pickup orders, the same four walls. Church increasingly became harder. Not because of what people said, but because of what they didn't say. The careful kindness that felt more like pity. The invitations that stopped coming. The slow, quiet way she'd been moved to the margins.

She wasn't looking for anything that Tuesday night. Just killing time in her car outside the dollar store, scrolling through her phone to avoid going inside where she might see someone she knew. She found a podcast someone had recommended months ago. She never made time for it, but that day she clicked—maybe just to feel like she was doing something spiritual. The speaker was talking about shame. About how Jesus doesn't wait for you to clean yourself up. How He spent a lot of time with women like her. How He knew their whole story and didn't flinch.

She'd heard it before, but this time was different. The words settled on her like a warm blanket on cold skin. *"He knows everything about me, and He stays."*

The words themselves didn't fix things, but they cracked something within. She didn't cry so much as exhale—a breath she didn't realize she'd been holding for years.

"I see you."

"I know what you've done."

"I'm not going anywhere."

It wasn't the kind of encounter people at church always talked about—no altar call, no tears on a pew. Just a quiet realization: God hadn't left; He was with her. He always had been.

She started listening more. Reading her bible again. Not out of obligation, but out of hunger. Her prayers weren't long—just fragmented thoughts. But they were honest. Something was shifting. She felt different. But not *that* different. It wasn't like anything dramatic had changed. She still had questions, still wrestled with regret, still lived in the same small town, still passed the same whispering faces in the grocery store parking lot.

But there was something quieter now. Lighter. Maybe it was peace. Maybe it was freedom.

It wasn't boldness. She didn't suddenly feel strong or "healed." But whatever it was—it showed. Because one day, a woman she only vaguely knew from town—a single mom going through her own slow-motion divorce—reached out. "I don't know why, but I feel like you'd understand. Can we talk?"

They met for coffee—two women with struggles to face and stories to tell. She just listened. Nodded. Told the truth about her own story as gently and plainly as she could.

As she shared, something shifted in her new friend's eyes. The guarded wariness melted into recognition, as if she'd been waiting her whole life to hear someone say, "You're not alone in this."

In the months that followed, their circle grew. More women reached out. Some through texts. Some through awkward, halting conversations in the corner of a church foyer. Women who had been hurt by the church, haunted by past choices, or silently surviving their own wilderness. She opened her living room. Put out folding chairs and lit a few candles. No plan, no curriculum. Just stories, tears, and prayers that didn't need to be polished.

They talked about Jesus—not the version who waited at the finish line, but the one who sat beside them in the mess. *"He met me at my worst. And He stayed."*

Slowly, word spread again. But this time, it wasn't gossip. It was grace. Even some of the women who had once kept their distance began showing up with their own stories to tell.

She still didn't think of herself as a leader. She still had bad days and second-guessed her worth. But she kept showing up. Kept pouring out whatever she had. Not because she was overflowing, but because something deeper had been planted in her—a spring that kept rising from the dry ground.

She wasn't fully healed. But she was honest. And in this wilderness life, sometimes honesty is the beginning of an oasis. It doesn't feel spectacular. It doesn't feel like leadership. It just feels like showing up with what little you have—and watching as God meets you there.

Leaking Vessels, Living Water

Maybe that's where you are right now. Still in process. Still afraid someone will see the cracks before they see the water. But listen—God uses thirsty people. He uses leaking vessels. He always has.

I've shared pieces of my own story—the mess, the brokenness, the long road of becoming. And somehow, in the middle of all of it, God still used me. Even when I wasn't whole. Even when I was still figuring things out, still stumbling forward with all kinds of contradictions in my heart—He let living water flow through me.

I watched friends come to faith—not because I had it all together, but because they saw something beginning to change in me. They caught a glimpse of the well springing up, and when I invited them to "come and see," they did. I served in our high school ministry—tech and video—while staff poured into my life.

Later, I worked with middle schoolers, pointing them to Jesus while wrestling to believe grace was mine. I landed an internship in college ministry, then eventually became staff—overseeing tech, then leading worship for the entire student ministry.

Yes, I was growing. Yes, I was repenting. Yes, I was slowly learning to put sin to death. But I was still in process. Still leaky. Still incomplete. And still—God used me to bring water to thirsty souls.

How insane is that? That we—fragile, flawed people—get to offer water in dry places. There's something amazing about walking through your own wilderness life and realizing that somehow, still, you can be a source of refreshment for others.

But this isn't about pretending everything's okay. That kind of image management—the pressure to look strong or whole—is like salt water. It looks refreshing, but the more you drink, the more parched you become.

The temptation is always there to offer polished words instead of honest ones. To show the version of ourselves that looks unshaken, even when the cracks are widening underneath.

But image management can't quench real thirst. The version of ourselves that has it all together, that never doubts or struggles—that polished, filtered testimony—can't create real connection. It builds walls instead of wells. Because what weary souls need isn't someone who looks whole. They need someone who knows what it is to thirst, and is willing to be seen anyway.

Walking through the wilderness should train us in honesty. It humbles us. It strips away the illusion of self-sufficiency. It teaches us how to live with tension—how to carry joy and sorrow, hope and exhaustion, longing and trust, all at once. And somehow, that kind of honesty creates space for grace to flow.

Because the gospel of Jesus really is absurd. It's wild enough that God would give His only Son to rescue us while we were still in rebellion—thirsty, cracked, and broken. But it doesn't stop there.

He doesn't just save us; he sends us. He entrusts us—fragile, flawed, still-in-process people—to carry His image into a broken and thirsty world.

And that's the miracle: We become water-bearers in the wilderness. Not because we're whole. Not because we have it all figured out. But because He is whole. And He is with us. Somehow, through all our cracks, His living water still flows.

Jesus' Way

The opening story of this chapter echoes one of the oldest and most beautiful moments in the New Testament. Long before that woman sat in her car outside a dollar store, wondering if grace could reach even her, another woman with a tangled past met Jesus at the most ordinary place in her world: a well.

She was a Samaritan. An outsider by ethnicity, by culture, by faith. A woman whose life was marked by broken relationships—five marriages, each one ending in loss, disappointment, or rejection. Now she lived with a man who wasn't her husband, a choice likely shaped more by survival than by love.

In her world, this meant shame. Public shame. Private shame. The kind that makes you take side streets to avoid familiar faces. The kind that clings to your name like dust. The kind that convinces you grace might be for other people—just not for you.

She came to the well alone. Not because it was convenient, but because it was noon—the hottest part of the day, when no one else would be there. Sometimes it's easier to sweat in the heat than to sweat beneath judgmental eyes. But that day, Jesus was already there. Waiting.

By every social rule, this moment should not have happened. A Jewish man—a rabbi, no less—alone with a Samaritan woman. Jews and Samaritans didn't speak. A man wasn't supposed to address a woman like this in public.

And this woman? Unclean. Heretic. Tainted by her past. She should have been dismissed. Ignored. But Jesus didn't just engage; He initiated. *"Will you give me a drink?"*

It seems like an offhand request, almost casual. But think about it: The Son of God, fully divine, fully human, allowed Himself to be thirsty. He didn't solve it with power. He didn't perform a miracle. No, He asked *her* for help. He led with vulnerability before ever addressing hers.

She was clearly caught off-guard. Her first response was laced with suspicion: *"You're a Jew and I'm a Samaritan woman. How can you ask me for a drink?"* (John 4:9). She braced herself, expecting another dismissal, another wound. She had learned to survive behind sarcasm and emotional armor.

But Jesus didn't correct her. He didn't sidestep her pain. He gently drew her in: *"If you knew the gift of God and who it is that asks you for a drink, you would have asked him and he would have given you living water"* (v. 10).

And then Jesus shifted. *"Go, call your husband and come back"* (v. 16).

A simple sentence—but so loaded. She hesitated. *"I have no husband"* (v. 17). It was technically true—but also a shield. A half-answer. A way to avoid going deeper. She knew where this conversation could go. She was used to questions turning into condemnation.

But Jesus didn't take the bait. He didn't shame her. He didn't corner her. He simply spoke the truth with gentle clarity: *"You are right when you say you have no husband. The fact is, you have had five husbands, and the man you now have is not your husband"* (v. 18).

He named her truth—not to expose her, but to invite her out of hiding. To show her: *Your thirst is what I came to satisfy.*

She pushed back—talking wells, ancestors, theology and where to worship. Underneath the diversion was someone who'd been told she didn't belong.

Jesus didn't dismiss her question. He met it directly: *"…a time is coming when you will worship the Father neither on this mountain nor in Jerusalem…true worshipers will worship the Father in the Spirit and in truth"* (vv. 21, 23). In other words: *"You're not disqualified. You're not excluded. The walls are coming down. The place doesn't matter anymore, your heart does."*

And something broke open in her. *"I know that Messiah is coming,"* she said. *"When he comes, he will explain everything to us"* (v. 25).

Jesus looked her in the eyes: *"I, the one speaking to you—I am He"* (v. 26).

Of all people in John's Gospel, this Samaritan woman with a shattered story was the first to hear: *"I'm the Messiah."*

Jesus knew her need wasn't about hydration; it was about healing. *"Everyone who drinks this water will be thirsty again, but whoever drinks the water I give them will never thirst,"* he said. *"Indeed, the water I give them will become in them a spring of water welling up to eternal life"* (vv.13–14).

Jesus wasn't offering her a better bucket—He was offering her a spring. Inviting her into a life that wouldn't have to be drawn up again and again through performance, striving, or shame. A life that would flow from within—unshaken by circumstances.

In an instant, she left her water jar behind—the very thing she had come for, her symbol of survival—and ran back to town. Something deeper had awakened: She had been seen, fully known, and still loved. And that love became her testimony.

She ran to the very people who had once shamed her, avoided her, defined her by her past—and declared: *"Come, see a man who told me everything I ever did!"* (v. 29).

Her scars became her sermon. Her past became her invitation. Her shame became her shout. And John tells us: Many believed because of her. Not because she had answers. Not because she was polished. But because she had been changed.

And here's the wildest part: She was still leaking. Still figuring it out. Still carrying scars. Still unfinished. And Jesus used her anyway.

Because this is how the Kingdom works. God doesn't wait for perfect vessels. He pours through cracked ones. The thirsty become fountains. The shamed become messengers. The exposed become free.

This was exactly what the prophets had already spoken. *"See, I am doing a new thing!…I am making a way in the wilderness and streams in the wasteland"* (Isaiah 43:19).

God doesn't wait for the ground to become fruitful first. He brings the water with Him. The wilderness itself becomes the place where life begins to break through.

That's what this woman did. She didn't wait to be whole. She didn't spend from abundance. She poured what she had—her story, her honesty, her transformation-in-process. And it was enough. She didn't have wealth or status or spiritual credentials. She had scars. She had a story. And she gave what she had.

This is the pattern of the Kingdom. The Way of Jesus. God doesn't wait for the cleaned-up. He doesn't only use the whole. He makes springs in wastelands. He turns former outcasts into fountains of living water.

This is why Paul was able to say, *"...I will boast all the more gladly about my weaknesses, so that Christ's power may rest on me"* (2 Corinthians 12:9). The more aware we are of our weakness, the more clearly His strength shines through.

And the early church understood this. They didn't lead from fullness or perfection. They simply *"devoted themselves to the apostles' teaching and to fellowship, to the breaking of bread and to prayer"* (Acts 2:42).

It wasn't polished or professional. But God moved. Their life together—simple, imperfect, dependent—became a well-watered garden in the middle of a weary world. The water was His. They merely showed up.

And yet, this invitation still feels terrifying to many of us. Because even now, the old lies start to taunt us:

I need to have it all together first.

I'm too inconsistent.

What if I mess it up?

I don't know enough. I'll hurt more than I help.

You've heard them. We all have. These are ancient lies. The enemy knows: If he can keep us waiting until we feel "ready," we may never pour at all. The longer we delay, the more the cracks feel disqualifying. The more our silence feels safer.

But Jesus doesn't wait for the perfect moment or the perfect vessel. He invites us to start here. Now. Leaky, cracked, and utterly dependent. Because His grace is enough to meet us—and to meet others through us.

You don't have to believe the lies. You don't have to be whole to pour. You just have to show up.

What Are We Waiting For

The woman at the well didn't go to seminary after her encounter with Jesus. As far as we know, she didn't clean up her past, reconcile every broken relationship, or prove herself spiritually mature before sharing what she had seen. She simply ran—still carrying the weight of her story—and told the truth about what Jesus had done.

What if we could see the struggle in our own unfinished stories the same way—not as disqualifications, but as testimonies in progress? It's not just a beautiful moment. It's a deeply instructive one. Because it reveals something essential about how the Kingdom of God works: God doesn't wait for resolution before He releases us. He pours through cracked vessels. And He always has.

But do you feel the tension? We hear stories like hers, we're moved by them—even stirred with hope—and then we quickly and quietly disqualify ourselves. We think, *I'm too broken.* Or, *I still need to work on me.*

We tell ourselves we'll serve after we've fixed this one part of our life…after we've cleaned up the mess.

So we sit on the sidelines. Not because we don't care—but because we feel unworthy. Too messy. Too incomplete. Too leaky to carry anything sacred.

But what if that's exactly where God wants to begin? That very sense of need—the awareness that you're not quite whole, not fully healed, still deeply dependent—isn't a barrier to being used. It's the doorway into the Kingdom.

All throughout Scripture, God chooses people who are in process. Moses was insecure and full of excuses, convinced someone else would do a better job. David was emotionally raw, morally compromised, and spent long stretches in the wilderness of his own making. Peter denied Jesus in

His most vulnerable moment and still became a pillar of the early church. None of them had it all together. And yet they were all chosen. All vessels. Leaky, cracked, wildly imperfect vessels through whom God poured out living water.

Because the Kingdom isn't built on polish. It's built on presence. Serving others—offering living water to those in dry places—isn't about arriving at spiritual maturity. It isn't about having a flawless testimony or theological precision. It's about showing up honestly and bringing what you have. Even when it feels small or fragile.

The truth is, we're all thirsty. We're all standing on the same ground—desperate for grace, longing for living water in a fractured and weary world. And maybe—just maybe—the scar you've been hiding is the very story someone else needs to hear. Maybe your in-process faith and your still-mending heart will open the door for someone else to believe that redemption is possible for them, too.

In the Kingdom of God, weakness isn't a liability—it's the language of love. And someone else might need to hear it spoken in your voice.

Still, this wilderness life has its own voice, too. It lies to us constantly. It whispers, *There's not enough. You'll never be enough.* It plants doubts in the quiet spaces: *If they really knew you, they wouldn't trust you. If they saw the cracks, they'd walk away.*

So we shrink back, believing a false gospel of scarcity and disqualification. We tell ourselves, *"I can't offer water when I'm this empty."*

But Jesus speaks a better word. He says, *"Look at the birds of the air. Look at the lilies of the field. Aren't you more valuable than these?"* (Matthew 6:26, 28, 30)

It's not a guilt trip. It's an invitation. You are not forgotten. You are not unseen. You are not too empty to be used. You don't have to be overflowing to offer a cup. You just have to be willing.

Yes, you may still feel broken. You may still be battling shame or uncertainty. You may be carrying grief, exhaustion, or unanswered questions. But none of that disqualifies you from being a vessel of grace. In fact, that's often where God does His most beautiful work—not in spite of the struggle, but right in the heart of it.

This doesn't mean bypassing your healing or ignoring the slow work of growth. It doesn't mean forcing yourself into leadership or pretending you're fine.

What it does mean is this: Being used by God isn't about being finished. It's about being honest. So don't wait until you're whole to offer water. Don't believe the lie that your mess disqualifies you. Bring what you have. Offer it in humility. And trust that the God who makes streams in the wasteland knows how to let living water flow through your cracks.

Never Ending, Overflowing

By now, I think we've dismantled the myth that you have to be whole to be used. We've named the lie that your weakness disqualifies you from offering water. But there's something even more surprising: Sometimes the very act of pouring out becomes the space where God meets you, too.

We don't give to get. This isn't transactional. But there is a strange, sacred mystery to it—something the woman at the well seemed to understand instinctively. She came empty and received something eternal. And in turning to offer it, she found herself more filled than when she began.

It doesn't always happen in the moment. Sometimes you won't feel it at all. Other times, when you least expect it, you'll find yourself sitting across from someone—offering a few stumbling words, a prayer you barely believe in, a presence you weren't sure you had the strength to give—and suddenly, the space between you feels holy. You realize: He's here. Not in a loud, miraculous way. Just present. With you. In you. Flowing through you.

There's a moment that's hard to explain until you've lived it: when you walk into a room feeling empty, and somehow—on the other side of showing up—you leave with more than you came in with. Not because you went looking for it. Not because that was the goal. But because in offering what little you had, you discovered that God was already there— meeting you in the very act of giving.

It's not about fixing anyone. It's not about solving suffering. And it's definitely not about filling your own tank by serving others. It's about showing up with what you have—your presence, your honesty, your scarred faith—and trusting that He will fill the space between your need and theirs. What's surprising is that sometimes, in the pouring out, you realize you've been filled too. Not because you earned it or because that's how it works. But because that's who He is.

Paul said it like this: *"...the God of all comfort...comforts us in all our troubles, so that we can comfort those in any trouble with the comfort we ourselves receive from God"* (2 Corinthians 1:3–4.).

And often, it's in the comforting—in the moment of pouring out—that we recognize just how much comfort we've personally received. Sometimes the clearest glimpse you get of Him is when someone else sees Him in you. When they thank you for a word you barely remember saying. When their tears fall and somehow your presence helps them breathe again. When you realize that, for a moment, your leaky cup carried living water. And you leave with no explanation except this: He was there.

But let's be clear: You won't always leave those moments feeling full. Sometimes you'll feel more tired. More aware of your own limits. That's okay. Being an oasis isn't about how refreshed you feel. It's about staying present. Trusting that even through your fatigue, His water still flows.

And that's why we need to remember: You don't have to wait to become an oasis. You don't have to be healed before you help. You don't need clarity before you offer comfort.

Being an oasis in the wilderness isn't about having all the answers. It's about being willing to stay with others in their pain. Not escaping it. Not conquering it. Not solving it. Just staying—honestly, tenderly, faithfully.

Jesus said, *"Let anyone who is thirsty come to me and drink... [and] rivers of living water will flow from within them"* (John 7:37–38). He didn't promise that our lives will overflow with ease or resolution. He promised that something deeper will rise up within. Something that moves through us even when the landscape around us is still barren.

You may not feel like a source of anything right now. I get it—there are many days I feel the same. You may still be grieving, doubting, or wondering what happened to the fire you once had. But hear this: The wilderness is not blocking your impact. It's the very place where it begins.

So where do you begin? You begin where you are—with what you have. You begin with presence. You begin with honesty. And you trust that it's more than enough. Not with grand gestures. Not with a plan to fix yourself first.

You begin small. Quietly. You begin by offering what's already in your hands—even if they tremble a little.

Maybe it looks like telling someone the truth about a scar you've carried—not to impress or to teach, but simply to say, "You're not alone."

Maybe it's reaching out to a friend who's hurting—not with perfect words, but with presence: "I don't know what to say, but I'm here."

Maybe it's checking in with someone regularly—not as a project, but as a fellow traveler.

Maybe it's showing up to serve in unseen ways—stacking chairs, writing a note, sitting beside someone in silence.

Or maybe it's praying out loud even when you feel uncertain, trusting that the Spirit often fills the spaces we feel most lacking.

You don't have to wait until you're overflowing to offer water. And you don't have to pretend you're not thirsty. You just have to show up—openhanded, honest, available. That's how living water flows.

So keep offering what you have. Keep showing up. Keep pouring. Not because you feel strong, but because you've met the One who is. And He is still flowing—through cracked vessels, in dry places, for the sake of others—and yes, even for you.

If you leave the conversation more tired than when you began, that's okay. Being an oasis doesn't mean you always feel refreshed. It means you trust that even through your fatigue, God's water still flows.

So don't wait. The world is full of thirsty people. Even in your weariness—even in your unfinished places—you carry something they need. You may not feel ready. You may not feel worthy. But if you know Jesus, the spring is already in you.

So go. Pour what you have. Trust the One who fills. And watch Him bring life to places you never thought possible.

11. The Long Way Home

Thriving With Hope on the Horizon

"I have told you these things, so that in me you may have peace. In this world you will have trouble. But take heart! I have overcome the world"
(John 16:33).

Why I Had to Write This

We started this book with my admission: I didn't want to write it.

Two weeks before my 50th birthday, I wanted to end my life. I was genuinely done—done with the confusion, frustration, failure, incompleteness. Done with waking up to another day that felt unbearable. I couldn't see a path forward. And I didn't want to see 51.

I had followed God for many years across multiple seasons. Through joy, pain, obedience, uncertainty. I had always given my full heart, energy, and time. Imperfectly, yes—but with passion and commitment. I had never been afraid to step out in faith, risk to see what God could do, move away from family, plant a church, step in and help revitalize a struggling church. I'm not risk-averse. (My wife is, but that's another book.)

I tried to listen closely to the Lord, obey when prompted, and stay faithful. And now, standing in the wreckage of what felt like monumental failure, I was overcome with loss, anxiety, shame, and the lingering fear that maybe God had abandoned me.

I've always been someone who could take a hit, shake it off, and get back up. I've always found the next thing, kept moving, kept building. But this time was different. The sense of calling that had once fueled me felt hollow. The clarity I'd built my life around was gone. The purpose that had anchored me seemed shattered. The hopelessness was foreign to me. The anxiety attacks were debilitating. I didn't recognize myself anymore.

That's how dark the wilderness became for me. And yet—ironically, it was in that darkness that something different started to grow. Not hope, at least not at first. Just this unsettling conviction that I couldn't ignore what I was feeling. I couldn't keep pretending. That maybe I needed to sit in the mess long enough to learn something new.

This book began in the *scubala* (Paul's not-so-subtle word for excrement) of that season. Wilderness living can suck. It's hard. It's disorienting. It's slow. It's part of the curse—the ground is hard, and life is painful. The thorns and thistles run deep. It's often one step forward and three steps back (with a kick to the groin added in for good measure). It grinds you down. It strips you of the illusion that life can be neatly managed or controlled. It makes you honest.

I didn't want to write this book; I *needed* to.

I needed to get honest about what this life really is, what God has (and hasn't) promised, and what it might look like to actually flourish—not in spite of the wilderness, but in the middle of it. I needed to wrestle with something I had preached and counseled for over twenty years.

I've always tried to teach out of what God was forming in me, not just what I could explain. But it's one thing to speak the truth and another thing entirely to wrestle with it when your own life is falling apart.

For me, the best way to wrestle has always been to write. So I did. I spent nearly a year showing up to the page almost daily—wrestling with God, with myself, with this wilderness life.

And yes, hopefully these pages will serve as a resource for others. I'd be grateful for that. But that's not why I wrote it. I wrote it for me. To survive. To process. To tell the truth.

Maybe you've seen your story somewhere in the pages of mine. Because this isn't a how-to. It's not a triumph story. It's a journey. I'm still becoming. And so are you. And as we come to this final chapter, I want to say it plainly: We still have a long way to go. But we do not walk it alone.

Ironically, the most freeing realization I've had is that this life is the wilderness. But that's not necessarily a bad thing; it's just reality. When we adjust our expectations—when we expect wilderness—we stop being so shocked by it. We stop seeing it as failure or punishment. We stop assuming that if we were stronger or more faithful, life would somehow feel easier. And we are free to start seeing God in it with us.

It's a paradox. Because for those who follow Jesus, this life is the worst it gets. This is the bottom of the barrel. Death, suffering, hatred, corruption, confusion—it's all here. The frustration that doesn't let up. The beauty that feels just out of reach. The longing that wakes you up in the middle of the night and follows you through the day.

And yet, there is still joy. There are beautiful things. The weddings. Graduations. Babies. Job promotions. There is laughter. There are moments of peace you didn't expect. Friendships that hold you together when your own faith can't. Glimpses of goodness that catch you off guard and remind you, He's here. Even here.

That's the strange thing about the wilderness. It wears you down, but it also grows things. Often without you even realizing it. And if you let it, the wilderness can shift something deep inside you. It can reframe everything.

This life isn't a mistake to be fixed. It's not a detour. It's not a punishment. It's the path. The wilderness is the place we're called to walk—not around, but through. And here's the hope: We do not walk it alone. God is here. Not watching from a distance. Not waiting on the other side. Right here. In it. With us. He has experienced the full weight of what this wilderness can do to a human being—the abuse, abandonment, betrayal, bleeding, silence, and the grave.

He didn't avoid it. He entered it fully. Which means He is not just a distant King. He is a sympathetic High Priest who doesn't merely understand us—He empathizes with us. He knows what it all feels like…because He has felt it all.

It doesn't erase the pain. It doesn't remove the longing. But it anchors us in the truth that even here—even now—we are not alone. We have a Savior who has gone before us, who is with us, and who speaks a better word over our weary hearts.

That's why, as we come to the words of Jesus in the Upper Room—words spoken to disciples who were about to face their own wilderness—we lean in. He doesn't sugarcoat it. He tells them exactly what is coming. And in doing so, He tells us, too.

Buckle Up Buttercup

Meeting with His disciples, Jesus didn't gloss over the truth. *"In this world you will have trouble. But take heart! I have overcome the world"* (John 16:33). He was as clear and direct as He could be, knowing exactly what was coming—for Him and for His disciples. The betrayal, the torture, the abandonment, the cross. Death itself.

And still, He looked them in the eye and said: "Take heart."

That wasn't a platitude. It was a command. A call to defiant courage in the face of real fear. An invitation to hold their ground when everything around them was about to fall apart. The disciples were just hours away from watching their world unravel. Jesus would soon be arrested, beaten, crucified. They would run, deny, hide, and fall apart. And Jesus knew it. And His encouragement to them was, "Take heart."

The Greek phrase here literally means "be of good courage" or "take courage." It's not passive comfort. It's an active command to summon courage in the face of overwhelming circumstances.

Even in the darkness, Jesus would remain who He had always been. In those words, Jesus was giving them something deeper than comfort—He was giving them an anchor. A truth to cling to when the waves hit. "Don't let the darkness make you forget who I am."

"Take heart" is stubborn hope. It's saying, "I'm not okay, but I'm not letting go." It's the spiritual equivalent of looking hell in the face and declaring, "You don't get the last word."

And for us? To take heart isn't about fake strength or grit-your-teeth religion. It's the unshakable courage that keeps showing up. Sometimes it's dragging yourself out of bed to pray when your faith feels paper-thin. Staying when it would be easier to run. Asking for help when everything in you screams to hide. Trusting when it feels impossible.

Jesus didn't say, "You *might* have trouble." He said, "You will."

It's not a warning. It's a promise—baked into the very experience of following Him in this wilderness life. Not because we're doing something wrong. Not because God is punishing us. But because this is what it means to live faithfully in a world still groaning for redemption. The wilderness is not an exception to the Christian life—it's the terrain of it.

So what exactly does it mean to "take heart" in the face of guaranteed trouble? It means that we have an anchor to hold onto when the wilderness kicks us in the teeth. Jesus declared, "I have overcome the world." Not *escaped*, but *overcome*.

He took every blow this world could throw—sin, shame, betrayal, grief. He let the wilderness crush Him, and then He rose. Scars on His body. Victory in His hands.

His triumph doesn't give us a shortcut around suffering—it means we don't walk through it alone. And the ending is already secure, even while we're still limping toward it.

This is what the writer of Hebrews meant when he declared: *"…we are receiving a kingdom that cannot be shaken"* (Hebrews 12:28).

Even here. Even in this mess. We are receiving it—not building it by effort, not earning it by faith. Receiving it. An unshakable Kingdom, already breaking through, even while the ground beneath us trembles.

This world is fragile. The wilderness can be brutal. But the Kingdom is not. It doesn't crumble when we fail. It doesn't dissolve when we doubt. It doesn't shift with the winds of culture or circumstance.

It stands: eternal, unbreakable, rooted in grace, held by the King who has overcome it all. So we take heart—not because we are strong, but because He is. We keep walking—not because this life is easy, but because this isn't the end. We hold on—not to the promise of comfort, but to the promise of His presence now and His Kingdom forever.

The promise is bigger than survival. *It's restoration.* A future so real, so physical, so final that it will make sense of every pain we've carried. A Kingdom so unshakable it won't just comfort our wounds—it will undo them.

This is what John saw in Revelation. He didn't see escape; he saw arrival. Heaven coming here. Home. "…Look! God's dwelling place is now among the people…" (Revelation 21:3).

Can you imagine it? Not just the end of external suffering. The healing of everything inside you that still feels unfinished. The low hum of discontent you can't explain. The shame you carry from wounds you never asked for. The frustration when your faith feels too small. The fractures in your soul that no one else can see, but you feel every day.

That brokenness will be made whole. Every anxious thought calmed. Every regret redeemed. Every splintered part of you—your mind, your memories, your identity—woven back together in peace.

This is the *shalom* we've longed for. Not just the absence of pain, but the presence of wholeness. To be fully known, fully healed—and finally, *finally*, at rest. "He will wipe every tear from their eyes. There will be no more death or mourning or crying or pain…" (Revelation 21:4). No more hiding. No more faking. No more trying to hold it all together.

That's what overcome means. Not just that Jesus made it through. But that He's coming to restore everything—around us and within us. He has overcome this world—and He is bringing His world with Him.

A home where nothing dies. Nothing breaks. Nothing separates us from the love of God. This is the hope that keeps us walking. Not that this wilderness won't cut us—but that it can't kill what He has already made alive. Not that our tears won't fall—but that not one of them will be wasted. Not that the pain isn't real—but that it isn't forever.

We don't just follow the One who survived the wilderness. We follow the One who is coming to end it. To dwell with us. To make all things new. To bring peace—not just to the world, but to *you*. And that's the future we are walking toward.

Living In-Between

We've been given a hope that cannot be shaken. We've been promised a Kingdom that will one day make all things new. Meanwhile, we are still here—in the in-between. The Kingdom is coming. The Kingdom is breaking through. But the wilderness is still the ground beneath our feet.

This middle place—this already-but-not-yet reality—shifts and moves like seasons. Whatever season you may be in right now—the stripped-back quiet of winter, the tentative stirring of spring, the overwhelming intensity of summer, or the letting-go of fall—the invitation remains the same: to receive the peace Jesus offers. Not peace as relief from the wilderness, but peace as His presence in it.

In the already-but-not-yet, we carry both the reality of present struggle and the promise of coming restoration. Both the ache of what is and the hope of what will be. We live with one foot in the Kingdom that is already breaking through and one foot in the wilderness that still surrounds us. It's the tension of being fully alive to both the beauty and the brutality of this life.

And in this tension, we discover something profound: We don't have to choose between acknowledging the pain and holding on to hope. We don't have to pretend everything is fine to maintain our faith. We don't have to have all the answers to trust God's heart. We can live honestly in the mess while clinging tenaciously to the promise that this isn't the end of the story.

And here, in this middle place, we still carry grief that doesn't heal the way we hoped. We lose people we love and never stop missing them. We walk through seasons where nothing gets better—where the breakthrough doesn't come, the healing doesn't arrive, the clarity never shows up.

Sometimes it's not a single moment of pain—it's a long ache drawn out over months, years. A weight you learn to carry, even when you're weary of carrying it. Here in the in-between death still has a sting, even if it is only temporary.

This life is the wilderness. And in it, there will be highs and lows, beauty and brokenness, gain and loss. There will be moments of joy that catch us by surprise—and long stretches of loneliness we never expected. There will be days when laughter comes easily, and days when even hope feels distant.

And yet—through it all—God walks with us. Not as a distant observer, but as an indwelling presence. He empowers us. He weeps with us. He speaks over us. He is our comforter, sustainer, protector, and Savior. There is joy and sorrow. Breakthrough and breakdown. Love and loss. In this wilderness life, they live side by side.

Jesus Himself didn't bypass the pain. In the garden, He cried out. He felt the weight of betrayal, the terror of what lay ahead. He sweat blood. He asked for another way. He didn't float above the agony; He entered it. He didn't numb Himself to the coming suffering; He faced it fully. And that's the God we follow. That's the anchor we cling to.

The Gospel is not a painkiller. It doesn't erase the ache or numb the heart. It is a foundation—steady and true—when nothing else holds. Not because life necessarily gets easier, but because He is faithful. That tension—that unresolved frustration we carry—is a sign we are still here. Still walking. Still breathing. Still in the story. And He is still in it with us.

That is what gives us courage to keep going. Because even in the uncertainty, God is not waiting for us to get it all together. He is not standing at the edge of the wilderness with arms crossed, waiting for us to pull ourselves out of the mud. He is not withholding His presence until our faith feels strong again. He meets us in the weakness. In the numbness. In the silence. In the long, dry stretches when we wonder if He is still paying attention. He is in it—right here, right now.

He came to walk it with us. To be the way through it. "I am the way, the truth, and the life." He is the way when you don't know the next step. He is the truth when everything else feels like chaos. He is the life even when everything around you feels like it's dying. And He doesn't just save your soul—He really is making all things new.

And that promise—"I am making all things new"—is what the Gospel is really about. It is personal, and it is cosmic. It is present, and it is still to come.

He is making your heart new—the places hardened by disappointment, the parts shut down by fear, the areas that forgot how to feel.

He is making your mind new—replacing old lies with new truth. Not erasing your past, but transforming how it defines you.

He is rebuilding your identity—not on what you've lost or what you've done, but on who you belong to.

He is renewing your relationships—teaching you how to forgive, how to trust again, how to love without armor.

He is breaking destructive patterns that once felt unchangeable.

He is restoring your sense of purpose—the part of you that still longs to matter.

And He is giving you back your peace—not the fragile kind that shatters under pressure, but the kind that holds even when everything else falls apart.

He is making this world new, too. Every torn place. Every buried injustice. Every inch of creation still groaning under the weight of what was lost. From deep systems of oppression to the quiet pain of a lonely kitchen table, He sees it all. And He is not just promising to restore it someday—He has already begun.

Here's the wild part: He is not just doing it cosmically. He is doing it through you.

You.

Yes, you—still tired, still waiting, still wounded. You are a place of shade for the weary. You are a vessel of living water for the thirsty. You are a quiet reminder to the world that God is still here and still working. He is making all things new—and He is starting with you. Right now. Right where you are.

Walking in the Way of Jesus

God isn't doing this work in isolation. He's using me for you, and you for me. Not only is God with us—closer than our very breath—but He has given us one another. Fellow wanderers. Brothers and sisters on the same long road. We are called to link arms, to lift up one another, to fight alongside each other as we journey toward the new heavens and new earth.

We are not just individuals trying to survive until heaven. We are a people—a community of Kingdom carriers—called to be living reminders that the best is yet to come. Together, we become an unlikely army of cracked vessels, pouring living water onto all the dry ground within our reach. This, too, is how the Kingdom breaks in—through us, together.

Think about what this means practically. When someone in your life is drowning in their wilderness season, you don't have to have all the answers. You just have to show up. You become the one who holds them up when they can't stand anymore. When you're the one who's struggling, you don't have to pretend you're strong. You can let others carry you for a while. This is how the body of Christ works—we take turns being strong for each other.

Kingdom carriers look different from wilderness survivors. Survivors hunker down, hoard resources, and wait for rescue. But Kingdom carriers? They pour out. They serve. They love lavishly, even in their own deficit. They create beauty in broken places. They speak hope over despair. They refuse to let others walk alone because they remember what it felt like to feel abandoned. They know that sometimes the most healing thing you can do in your wilderness is to walk with someone in theirs.

This is why community isn't optional for followers of Jesus. We were made for each other. Designed to carry each other's burdens. Called to spur one another on toward love and good deeds. In a world that teaches us to be self-sufficient and independent, the church offers something countercultural: *interdependence*. The radical idea that we need each other not just for company, but for survival. For formation. For the kind of love that changes the world.

This Kingdom isn't some distant future. It's already breaking through—in quiet, sacred, almost imperceptible ways. In acts of forgiveness that shouldn't make sense. In meals shared between people who once stood on opposite sides. In the stillness you feel when you finally stop striving and just breathe. In the small moments of grace that catch you off guard and remind you: He's here. We don't have to wait for heaven to experience His presence. Heaven is already moving in.

This is the Gospel: God came down into the wilderness to find us—we don't have to climb our way to Him. Not that everything gets fixed overnight, but that nothing is wasted. Not that suffering is erased, but that He enters it—and is transforming it from the inside out. He is making all things new. Even you.

And this life? Yes, it's still the wilderness. It always will be—on this side of Eden. We all live east of the garden in a world still groaning for redemption. But that is not failure. That is not a flaw in the plan. It's reality. And it is not without meaning.

This wilderness life is formative. God uses it. He leverages every ache, every longing, every loss to shape us, refine us, reveal Himself in ways comfort never could. The wilderness is not wasted. And the hard seasons are not signs of His anger or absence. They never have been.

He is present—closer than breath. The cloud by day. The fire by night. The Shepherd who leads. The Father who loves. The Spirit who indwells. Always.

And so we keep walking. Not because we are strong. Not because we have all the answers. But because Jesus is the way through this wilderness. The way, the truth, the life. He has walked it before us. He walks it beside us. His Spirit lives within us. And we do not walk alone. We have Him. And we have each other—fellow wanderers, fellow image-bearers, fellow vessels of grace. This is how the Kingdom breaks in—through Him, through us, together.

This long way home is not about the distance left to travel. It's about the companionship we've been given for the journey. The wilderness isn't punishment; it's preparation. The waiting isn't wasted; it's formative. The struggle isn't a sign of God's absence; it's the very place He does His deepest work. When we see our unfinished stories not as evidence of failure, but as chapters still being written by the Author of hope, everything changes.

The Promised Land may not be here yet. But the Kingdom is breaking through. And we are walking toward it together, sustained by the One who has already walked this road and overcome. This is the truth that changes everything: We are not wilderness survivors. We are Kingdom carriers—living reminders that the best is yet to come.

What Now?

So what does this actually look like? How do we live as Kingdom carriers instead of wilderness survivors? How do we shift from merely enduring to actively thriving with hope on the horizon?

It starts with how we see ourselves:

Wilderness survivors focus on getting through. Kingdom carriers focus on giving away.

Survivors ask, "How long will this last?" Kingdom carriers ask, "How can I love well right here?"

Survivors hunker down and wait. Kingdom carriers look around and serve.

It shows up in how we treat our pain. Instead of hiding our struggles or pretending they don't exist, we let them become bridges to others who are hurting. We stop seeing our scars as disqualifications and start seeing them as credentials. We realize that our deepest wounds often become our greatest ministry. Not because we have all the answers, but because we know what it feels like to need grace.

It changes how we respond to others when they are in particularly difficult wilderness stretches. Instead of offering quick fixes or spiritual platitudes, we offer presence. We show up. We sit in the mess. We bring meals and ask follow-up questions and remember anniversaries of loss. We become living reminders that they are not walking alone.

Kingdom carriers learn to hold both grief and gratitude, longing and contentment, struggle and joy. They don't wait until their problems are solved to start serving others. They don't put their lives on hold until they feel "ready." They pour out what they have, trusting that God multiplies weak offerings.

This week, look around. Who in your life is in a wilderness season?

Maybe it's your neighbor dealing with a diagnosis. A coworker going through a divorce. A friend whose child is struggling. A family member battling depression. You don't have to fix them. You just need to see them. And refuse to let them walk alone.

When you're in a challenging season, remember this: You are not just surviving. You are being prepared. Shaped. Refined. God is doing something in you through the struggle that He couldn't do in the comfort.

So walk boldly. Walk honestly. Walk sacrificially. Lean in to Him. Lean in to each other. Don't give up. Don't give in. And remember this: One day, you will hear, "Well done, good and faithful servant." One day, you will see the Promised Land with your own eyes. You will stand in the presence of the One who walked the wilderness for you and with you. And every weary step will have been worth it.

But until that day—we walk. Together. In hope. In faith. In Him. And that's not just survival, it's thriving with hope on the horizon.

Epilogue

This is real love—not that we loved God, but that he loved us and sent his Son as a sacrifice to take away our sins. Dear friends, since God loved us that much, we surely ought to love each other (1 John 4:10-11, NLT).

When I finished the last chapter of this book, I thought I was done. Done wrestling with these words, done sitting with these stories, done trying to articulate what it means to live between tension and trust. But the wilderness has a way of offering one more lesson when you least expect it.

As I was scrolling through social media (I know, there are better things I should be doing with my time), I saw his face. The founding pastor of the church where I used to work. The one whose moral failure created an implosion that sent shockwaves through hundreds of lives. The one whose choices left wounds that still haven't fully healed.

My first instinct was familiar and ugly: Screenshot it, send it to a friend, indulge in that brief hit of righteous curiosity that comes from glimpsing someone else's story. The old me would have done it without thinking twice. *Look at this! He and his family—look, they had a child.*

But something different happened instead. Standing there in my kitchen, staring at his picture, I felt something I didn't expect: *compassion*. Not the kind that makes excuses or minimizes harm, but the kind that recognizes shared brokenness. The kind that sees a fellow human being who has carried the weight of his failures for more than a decade now. The kind that acknowledges a simple truth: I am no better than he is. He is no more broken than I am.

Life in the wilderness had changed something in me.

This is what I couldn't have told you when I started writing this book—that the wilderness doesn't just teach you how to endure your own mess. It teaches you how to see everyone else's mess differently, too.

It strips away the illusion that some people are beyond hope and others are beyond failure. It levels the playing field in the most uncomfortable and beautiful way possible.

Living in the wilderness—really living in it, not just surviving it—grows things in you that prosperity never could. Patience with your own slow progress. Grace for other people's spectacular failures. A deep, bone-level understanding that we are all just walking each other home, stumbling over roots and rocks, occasionally catching each other when we fall.

The truth is, we're all in this together. Every single one of us is carrying something. Fighting something. Grieving something. Hoping for something. The wilderness doesn't play favorites—it strips us all down to what's real.

We have a choice: We can either continue to weaponize the wilderness with each other—using our pain as proof of someone else's failure and our struggles as ammunition for judgment—or we can become traveling companions, people who recognize that everyone limping through this terrain deserves grace, not condemnation.

The wilderness shifts everything—including how we see the people who have hurt us, disappointed us, let us down. It doesn't erase the harm or excuse the choices, but it makes room for the possibility that redemption is bigger than our wounds, that grace is more powerful than our grievances, that no one—not even the ones who have caused the most damage—is beyond the reach of God's healing love.

I never would have believed that ten years ago. Five years ago. Maybe not even a few months ago as I typed the final words of this book. The wilderness keeps teaching, keeps forming, keeps shifting the way we see and the way we love.

So here's what I want to leave you with, what the wilderness has been whispering to me all along: You are not who your worst moment says you are—and neither is anyone else. The failures that feel final aren't. The wounds that feel permanent can heal. The people who feel unforgivable aren't.

The wilderness is still the terrain we walk, still the space between rescue and home. But it's also the place where grace grows deep roots, where compassion learns to flourish in impossible soil, where broken people discover they can still be conduits of God's redemptive love.

We still have a long way to go. All of us. And sometimes—on the good days, in the unexpected moments, when grace catches us off guard—we remember that the One who walks with us specializes in making all things new. Even the things that look beyond repair. Even the people we thought were beyond hope.

Even us.

The wilderness changes everything. And in the end, that might be the most beautiful gift of all.

An Invitation

If this book met you somewhere in the wilderness,
I'd love to keep walking with you.

I share reflections, stories, and new projects at dustinkleinschmidt.com
and through my Substack newsletter, *The Wilderness Way*.

You can also find resources, conversations,
and updates about future books at thenormalpastor.com.

Wherever you are on the journey—keep walking. You're not alone.

SCRIPTURE REFERENCES

OLD TESTAMENT

Genesis 2:18; 3; 3:17–19

Exodus 13:17–18; 16:2–8; 17; 19:5–6; 32

Numbers 11; 13–14

Deuteronomy 8:2–5

1 Samuel 16–31

2 Samuel 11–12

1 Kings 18:27; 19:1–18

2 Kings 23

Job 1–2; 38–42

Psalms 6:6; 13:1–2; 32:3–5; 34:18; 42:6–7, 11; 46:10; 63:2–8; 78:14–20; 84:5–7

Proverbs 3:5–7

Ecclesiastes 3:1–7; 4:1–3

Isaiah 24:4–6; 30:15, 18; 32:17–18; 43:18–19; 48:10; 55:11; 58:10–11

Jeremiah 7:31; 17:9

Hosea 2:14–15

Lamentations 3:19–22

NEW TESTAMENT

Matthew 3:17; 4:1–11; 5:45; 6:26, 28, 30; 7:13–14; 11:28–29; 25:23; 26:38–39

Luke 10:38–42; 22:42–44

John 4:9–10, 13–18, 25–29; 7:37–38; 10:27; 14:27; 15:5; 16:33; 19:26–27

Acts 2:42; 3:6

Romans 5:3–5; 8:18–28, 32

1 Corinthians 10:3–5

2 Corinthians 1:3–4; 4:7–9, 16–18; 5:2–5; 10:3–5; 12:7–10

Galatians 3:3

Ephesians 4:3

Philippians 3:20; 4:7

1 Thessalonians 2:8

Hebrews 2:10; 3:7–19; 5:8; 10:23–25; 11:13–16; 12:1–2, 7, 28

James 1:2–4; 5:7

1 Peter 1:6–7; 5:8–9

1 John 4:10–11

Revelation 21:1–5

About the Author

Dustin Kleinschmidt grew up in Los Angeles and met Jesus in high school. Like many things in his life (including writing this book), he kind of fell forward into ministry. Over two decades later, he continues to help others navigate the tensions of faith, formation, and everyday life through writing, coaching, and creative work.

He lives in Texas with his wife, Stacy, and their kids. You can follow his writing and reflections at "The Wilderness Way" on Substack or visit dustinkleinschmidt.com.

ACKNOWLEDGMENTS

There are too many people to name who helped shape this book and the journey behind it, but a few deserve special mention.

To **Richard Reising**—friend, mentor, and super-smart dude. Over and over, you've helped me clarify the heart and vision God has given me—not just for this book but for the work ahead. Your wisdom and belief have mattered deeply. I love your optimism (even if I don't always trust it).

To **Carol Stertzer**—thank you for the care, insight, and steady encouragement you brought to this project. When I wasn't sure if what I had was any good, you reminded me that it was worth the work. You helped me see this book more clearly than I could have on my own and gave me the confidence to keep going.

To **Keith Spurgin**—thank you for being both a pastor and a friend through many seasons. You've been one of the few who quietly and faithfully serve Jesus' church without the press or the perks, and I'm grateful to still be walking alongside you.

To **Brad Sarian**—there aren't many people I look forward to Zoom calls with, but you're one of them. Thank you for your friendship and for the way you model Jesus as a pastor and a friend.

To **Dean Yorimitsu**—thank you for bringing your creativity to this project and for your love for Jesus that shines through your work.

And to everyone who encouraged, prayed, and believed in this message—you've been part of the wilderness with me.

NON-BIBLICAL CITATIONS

Angelou, Maya. 2008. *Letter to My Daughter.* New York: Random House.

Bennington, Chester. 2017. "Chester Bennington Discusses Dark Thought That Inspired 'Heavy.'" *Loudwire,* July 21, 2017.

Hauerwas, Stanley. 1997. *Wilderness Wanderings: Probing Twentieth-Century Theology and Philosophy.* Boulder, CO: Westview Press.

Jordan, Michael. 1994. *I Can't Accept Not Trying: Michael Jordan on the Pursuit of Excellence.* San Francisco: HarperSanFrancisco.

Keller, Timothy. 2004. "Marriage as Friendship." Sermon on Genesis 2:18. Redeemer Presbyterian Church, New York, NY. Accessed September 30, 2025, from *Gospel in Life.*

Lasso, Ted. 2020. Season 1. Apple TV+. Created by Bill Lawrence, Jason Sudeikis, Joe Kelly, and Brendan Hunt.

McKelvey, Douglas Kaine. 2017. *Every Moment Holy, Volume I.* Franklin, TN: Rabbit Room Press.

Nouwen, Henri J. M. 2004. *Turn My Mourning into Dancing.* Nashville: Thomas Nelson.

Teresa of Calcutta. 2007. *Come Be My Light: The Private Writings of the "Saint of Calcutta."* Edited by Brian Kolodiejchuk. New York: Doubleday.

Tolkien, J.R.R. 1954. *The Fellowship of the Ring.* London: George Allen & Unwin.

Cohen, Leonard. 1992. "Anthem." Track 5 on *The Future.* Columbia Records.

www.ingramcontent.com/pod-product-compliance
Lightning Source LLC
Chambersburg PA
CBHW060353110426
42743CB00036B/2846